WORLD AFFAIRS — A Prophetic Preview

Many of the cycles we now enter, most notably those related to the planets Pluto and Uranus, are extremely long in duration. In the distant future, these are very useful to the world, but for now we have to content ourselves with less protracted influences, and ones that, though showing some temporary improvement, cannot be seen as being entirely helpful.

World watchers need careful eyes during 1996, for so many potentials are breeding beneath the surface of the pond that it would be easy to miss them. For example, religious fundamentalism thrives in all parts of the globe, threatening peace and stability later. Large nation states are looking to their own internal needs, and often missing more widespread facts that need dealing with at source. Islam, as always, is misunderstood in the West, and the emergence of a new 'Mahdi' type figure is likely. A greater desire to understand the Muslim mind now could avoid much grief later.

GREAT BRITAIN

Almost from the start of the year, disposable income is rising. With political trends still very changeable, any thoughts of an election are likely to wait until late in the year. In fact, astrologically speaking, the first part of 1997 is a far more likely time for the government to go to the country. The fortunes of the Conservative Party fluctuate. By late summer indications of yet more serious splits are more or less inevitable and the future of the Prime Minister is in some severe doubt. Meanwhile, money markets fluctuate, though they do show more stability in Britain than in some other parts of Europe.

Opposition parties appear to have far more in common now, and any competition between them is more likely to be based on the feeling of 'personality cults', rather than on any fundamental disagreements in policy. Alliances are unwritten, though in the minds of pundits, and in reality, they do exist. Aside from this, the Labour Party shows itself as stronger and more cohesive. Its leader is becoming a statesman to be reckoned with and, after changes early in the year, the shadow cabinet also looks secure and capable. Many political watchers now consider that here we have a true 'government in waiting'.

Trends that indicate a significant change in circumstances for HRH The Prince of Wales are also at their most potent towards the end of the summer, indicating a more complete marital separation and even a public commitment to a new union. Meanwhile, other members of the Royal Family appear to be keeping a lower profile than of late. Transits appearing in the charts of specific royals are few and far between, so that silence, imposed or self imposed, can be expected. However, constitutional questions are still being asked and the whole issue of the monarchy is once again up for public debate. The Queen may be seen to capitulate over a particularly contentious issue early in the autumn.

Northern Ireland is a great focus of attention throughout much of the year, and the astrological trends relating to this part of Britain during 1996 tend to indicate that the peace process is now beyond doubt, even if protracted negotiations, hedging and bargaining, delay the general aspirations of the populace. Other aspects for Britain indicate cuts in the armed services, which might again propose a lull in violence within Northern Ireland. Any constitutional changes are most likely to emerge late in the year.

PUBLISHED IN JUNE 1995

THE TITLE, STYLE OF MAKE-UP AND CONTENTS OF THIS ALMANACK ARE STRICTLY COPYRIGHT

FOULSHAM'S
ORIGINAL MOORE'S
ALMANACK

1697 *THE ORIGINAL COPYRIGHT EDITION* **1996**

1996: Business and Determination

The year of 1996 brings a whole host of powerful cycles. For the astrologically minded these include Pluto's movement into Sagittarius, Uranus' entry into Aquarius, and the approaching trough in the sunspot cycle, which itself can bring some significant changes in world affairs. The most important immediate trend however is Jupiter's passage through Capricorn.

We should see the world economic situation improving, even though the contradictory trends might make this possibility less evident in a month by month sense. Confidence will wax and wane, whilst the more distant trends remain fairly certain.

Beware investors! Speculations of a long duration, world wide, are more likely to prosper, and those who commit themselves to potential immediate gains are liable to come severely unstuck. The area for overall success pivots in the direction of German and Japanese markets, whilst our own British markets are steady, though less impressive. The United States of America will fluctuate wildly from an economic view-point.

The forces of law and order are definitely in evidence throughout the year, a fact that is as evident in everyday life as it turns out to be with established financial institutions, which are clamping down severely on those who, through greed or lawlessness, would bring financiers and bankers into disrepute. Predictions of a general market crash around August will not materialise, though this is the most tenuous time for would-be investors. During this part of the year, and again in October, success comes to those who remain calm and who do not allow themselves to give way to unnecessary panic.

Tel. (01753) 526769

Jupiter's movements especially are almost certain to bring moments of extreme tension, even if many of these, and especially the ones that are strongest in August and October, are also replays of past events. There will be a new ordering of world powers, evident throughout the whole year, which is most obvious in the case of the USA, Russia and Europe. All authorities will be trying to strengthen the UN, even if each nation state has its own ideas about what the role of this body should actually be. 1996 may begin a long period of self-appraisal for the UN, with new methods of financing its efforts being discussed and perhaps demands for a greater degree of involvement and decision making from the third world.

In a more local sense, the same planetary movements have a bearing on the EEC, where all is not well. France and Germany can expect civil problems at home, creating a political atmosphere in which it is difficult for governments to react strongly. Britain, on the other hand, is more stable and the government fairly decisive, a fact that can also reflect in our own economic position, since stability creates confidence. However, the EEC could suffer, with most European eyes taking on a nationalistic stare, each toward his capital and away from the union.

Historically speaking, we can say much by looking at previous sunspot cycles which, with their eleven year beat pattern, approach their lowest count in 1996 and 1997. The sunspot trough is almost always accompanied by a period of greater peace and stability world-wide, a fact that indicates some breathing space from global problems. One word of caution however is that such a trough often shows deeply nationalistic states, though quiet, preparing themselves for a more expansionist stage later, and with this regard, world eyes should be focused on Russia.

Progressive thinkers are much in evidence during 1966 and so new political and economic models are being suggested. Although communism itself may be dead, a close relative is coming to birth. We see the promise of a second 'cold war', even if this comes somewhat further down the line. If the world is sensible, there are parallels from earlier this century that should not be ignored. For 1996 though, if there is such a thing as a 'feel good factor' at a global level, perhaps the year that lies before us shows something of its potential to improve optimism and help the world to look forward positively.

The Tarot trump for 1996 is 7 (i.e. 1+9+9+6=25; 2+5=7) and is the Conqueror. This suggests intense international competition, and also competition on the sports tracks and in other fields, with many records being broken. This is a year when we will all be encouraged to exceed our own personal best, and with cooperation on board too, it is a year of hope.

Old Moore wishes all his readers a peaceful, happy and prosperous year ahead.

Old Moore, December 1994

In sporting terms British competitors are likely to do well in a number of different disciplines, and this estimation would fall well in line with a rising feeling of 'nationalism' which although not particularly evident in the British heart as a rule proves to be more so in 1996. Partly because of this fact, doubts concerning the EEC do continue to grow and multiply. From the position of asking what can be done to rectify problems in this area, more and more voices, some of them very influential ones, are calling for radical solutions. Most citizens of the UK do find some improvements evident in their lives during 1996, though changes for the better are slow and often painful, so that a broad overview is required.

THE UNITED STATES

It is, of course, election year in the United States of America, and the event is likely to take place on November 5th. This is not a good time, since astrological trends indicate troubles, or crimes that threaten the government. This suggests that President Clinton's past mistakes may well have caught up with him. The mood of the people favours a Republican victory and, ahead of the election, President Clinton's personal chart is so weak that he may not even achieve inauguration.

Paradoxically, in the first half of the year at least, there are indications of greater optimism economically, which under circumstances prevailing at the time could easily lead to a frantic, but misleading, consumer boom. After July things change however, suggesting economic difficulties, and very late in the year foreign policy gaffes are also extremely likely.

ELSEWHERE IN THE WORLD

A somewhat more quiet year for Russia is likely, as the 'Bear' shows a more introspective period than of late. The West should beware, because all is not as it appears and there are factions within the country that can, and will, cause problems in the fullness of time, if they are not opposed at source by democratic forces. Public opinion is not generally on the side of sensible reform and border disputes with yet more former satellite states are inevitable.

In the Balkans we find the seeds of yet greater disasters being sown, as the general problems attending the area threaten to spread to Macedonia and Albania. In the case of the former, the danger comes from a more aggressive Greece becoming involved in the situation. We look to a year of constant threats, counter threats and posturing, with Old Moore seeing 1997 as the more likely focus for these problems.

Japan alone looks set fair for a period of relative stability, and new innovations at regular intervals show the Rising Sun continuing to achieve economically what its military adventures of the 1940's could not achieve. Many states in the Pacific and beyond bow the fiscal knee to Japan, where nationalistic elements may be showing a rather menacing, though abortive, presence in domestic politics.

The Middle East brings few surprises, not least of all great conflict within the political structure of Israel, where all the way through the year there may be ferocious arguments between moderates and Zionists. Jordan is also a focus of interest, probably as a result of changing political fortunes for its Royal Family. February, June and August are the foci of difficulties in the case of both states. Civil insurrection in Bahrain, and a possible change in government, though seeming improbable, does look likely.

TONY BLAIR

Tony Blair is a man of the moment, a new breed Labour politician who has been described as "a live wire, an intellectual dynamo, open-minded, creative, constantly on the move". Many are pinning their hopes on Tony Blair's commitment to re-inventing his party and winning the next election. Where does his drive come from?

Blair was born in Edinburgh on May 6th, 1953, at 6:10 am. This makes him a Taurean with Gemini rising, and the Moon in diplomatic Aquarius. This is a decidedly intellectual combination but one that is also practical, consistent: he can back up his rhetoric and high ideals with hard work. Taurus is an earth sign and values material stability. As a Sun Taurus, therefore, Blair is naturally in touch with reality, meaning *the basic human need for adequate food, shelter, and satisfying work.* In his birth-chart we also find Jupiter in Taurus, indicating an expansion of the Taurus principle. Mars close by, in Gemini, and exactly with his Ascendant, strengthens his resolve and the power of his verbal expression. Jupiter in Taurus gives him a generous but moderate nature, and a deep appreciation of the good life, in all senses of the word. This is the mark of someone who, having achieved security and material well-being, can take it for granted and so direct his energies freely in cultural and socio-political channels. But Jupiter's house placement is even *more* revealing: in the powerful angular position, just above the Ascendant, it symbolises *the successful politician,* the philanthropist who aspires to bring humanitarian values down to earth and put them to use in a productive way.

Blair's elevated Moon in Aquarius has something to do with this, too. As a born humanitarian and an instinctive social theorist, Blair is genuinely concerned about steering a *morally sound* course, one that both empowers and supports his fellow man. Inwardly he feels himself to be a friend of the world, dedicated to humane principles and motivated to becoming a great force for good. The Moon in the 10th, and with fine aspects to Venus, Mars and the Ascendant, insures popularity, versatility and social grace. Describing Blair as a "social conservative" is an astrologically accurate blend of Taurus and Aquarius: his lunar side goes for caring socialism, but that stalwart Sun in Taurus knows that *opportunity* must be matched by *responsibility.* With Sun square Pluto, the expression of his *essential nature* (the Sun) will inevitably require the burial and/or transformation (Pluto) of certain Socialist policies that shackle the party to the past. A favourable aspect from Uranus reveals a talent for positive change and for the 'create and adjust" policy that succeeds in re-inventing the new from the old.

Blair has Saturn conjunct Neptune so he is a practical visionary, and his vision can recapture the essence of Labour's principles if he does not lose force by focusing on details prematurely. As Uranus moves into Aquarius (early in '96) and Pluto just into Sagittarius opposes his Mars and Ascendant ('96-'97), Blair seems set to stay in the forefront of British politics. Antagonism from 'fundamentalists' within his party is likely, and the burden of trying to solve too many problems too fast will be keenly felt. But Blair has Taurean staying power; another way to put it: he's courageous and stubborn, and it's unlikely that he will let go of his belief that "opportunity and obligation go together".

Your 1996 Birthday

YOUR PERSONAL FORTUNE AND GUIDE

One of the following monthly readings is **PERSONAL TO YOU. Good days
for Romance, Business, Finance, Travel and Social Affairs.** Each monthly
forecast gives both your general and actual Birthday fortune for 1996 as well as

YOUR PLANETS, BIRTHSTONE AND YOUR LUCKY DAY

 ## CAPRICORN BORN PEOPLE

**Birthdays between December 22nd and January 20th inclusive.
Your planet is Saturn. Birthstone, garnet. Lucky day, Saturday.**

SUN–MOON CYCLES: All astrology depends on cycles, and at the end of each month in the readings
below, you will find a series of diary dates, each connected with the commencement of a two-day cycle that
relates to the moving Moon and its association with your Sun sign. The dates listed are headed **Love,
Fortune, Health** and **Recharge**. The first three indicate times when effort really pays out in the area
concerned, whilst **Recharge** means putting in less effort and taking a break from pressure.

JANUARY   A good enough start to the year, especially considering that you are now working hard and
are able to make life work out practically. Not all your endeavours are positive however, and some regard to
changing patterns in love could make January a month of minor personal arguments. Late in the month,
look out for money that comes from some fairly surprising directions.
Love 13, 14. Fortune 19, 20. Health 26, 27. Recharge 5, 6.

FEBRUARY   Your main objective in February is to put right difficulties from the past and to use much of
the month to build a new and more interesting series of possibilities for the future. Confidence grows in line
with your Capricorn ability to get things done in a practical sense, but there are areas of your life which take
a back seat. Family matters may be one of them.
Love 9, 10. Fortune 17, 18. Health 25, 26. Recharge 3, 4.

MARCH   The great and good seem to enter your life at present, bringing with them confidence in your
abilities and probably persuading you that you have more and greater potential than you had thought. As
the month goes on you should find the most noticeable cycles are related to the way you get on with others.
Good and bad, you can't get away from relationships this month.
Love 9, 10. Fortune 17, 18. Health 24, 25. Recharge 3, 4.

APRIL   Anxiety needs to be put to the back of your mind as much as you find to be possible during April.
For one thing, there is too much to be done to worry about inconsequential details and in any case, fretting
just doesn't help at all. In terms of progress in personal attachments, the trends look especially good –
though towards the end of the month, and after a rather more shaky start.
Love 7, 8. Fortune 15, 16. Health 22, 23. Recharge 1, 2.

CAPRICORN BORN PEOPLE

MAY Not everyone might have your best interests at heart, though you have to remember that some of this might be down to the way your own mind is working. Some positive cycles commence now, and can take your mind away from too much self-analysis. Concentrate particularly on travel, adventure and the chance to broaden your horizons away from the confines of everyday life.
Love 5, 6. Fortune 13, 14. Health 21, 22. Recharge 30, 31.

JUNE The first of the genuine summer months finds you feeling a great deal more optimistic about life in general than your naturally sceptical sign is sometimes inclined to do. As a result, you might decide to push more energy this month in the direction of your career, which, with effort, could easily be improving. Once again you need to create more personal space.
Love 4, 5. Fortune 11, 12. Health 19, 20. Recharge 28, 29.

JULY The second half of the year finds you looking forward to celebrations, many of which you participate in creating yourself. Such are the personal trends you encounter during July, that almost anything practical you undertake shows a greater chance of working out to your satisfaction. You might occasionally feel a tool of fate, but remember – the choices are yours.
Love 2, 3. Fortune 9, 10. Health 17, 18. Recharge 27, 28.

AUGUST Right and wrong are concepts that you hold to be very important. Aspects in your chart now show that you are more keen than ever to tell the difference between the two. Potential for travel shows again just how expansive Capricorn can be just at the moment, so that even if you find circumstances keeping you in one place physically, the month is very good for flights of fancy.
Love 1, 2. Fortune 7, 8. Health 15, 16. Recharge 26, 27.

SEPTEMBER You really are worth a great deal more in the eyes of the world than you sometimes consider yourself to be, and you can spend at least part of September coming to terms with the fact. It should not be hard, because if anything sets this period apart, it's the recognition of your own importance to others. Look out some new types of entertainment and in sport, go for gold.
Love 1, 2. Fortune 5, 6. Health 13, 14. Recharge 24, 25.

OCTOBER It's back to basics as far as Capricorn is concerned right now. You want to get the best out of your capabilities, but might have to look deep inside your own nature and in some cases, start from scratch. There is nothing at all wrong with admitting that you sometimes need help, and you face a world that is more than willing to put itself out on your behalf now.
Love 29, 30. Fortune 3, 4. Health 11, 12. Recharge 22, 23.

NOVEMBER As the Sun moves slowly and surely back to your own part of the zodiac, so your tendency towards good luck is on the increase. This turns out to be the best month for chancing your arm in some way, and particularly when dealing with subject matter that you really understand. Realism is not difficult to establish, but you need the occasional bout of silliness too!
Love 27, 28. Fortune 3, 4. Health 12, 13. Recharge 20, 21.

DECEMBER In almost every sphere of your life, actions speak louder than words this December. Some of your efforts at the beginning of the month are geared towards the Christmas period, or at least they should be. Rules and regulations are almost certain to get on your nerves, though it is doubtful that you will find a way round them. Some humour would help most.
Love 25, 26. Fortune 1, 2. Health 9, 10. Recharge 19, 20.

.. 12 ..

AQUARIUS BORN PEOPLE

Birthdays between January 21st and February 19th inclusive. Your planets are Saturn and Uranus. Birthstone, amethyst. Lucky day, Saturday.

SUN–MOON CYCLES: All astrology depends on cycles, and at the end of each month in the readings below, you will find a series of diary dates, each connected with the commencement of a two-day cycle that relates to the moving Moon and its association with your Sun sign. The dates listed are headed **Love, Fortune, Health** and **Recharge**. The first three indicate times when effort really pays out in the area concerned, whilst **Recharge** means putting in less effort and taking a break from pressure.

JANUARY   Yours is a unique and quite original sort of sign, a fact that shows from the word go as far as January is concerned. Do your best to let your bright and cheerful optimism shine out and you really can't go far wrong. This is not to suggest that you will get quite the reaction that you are after from everyone, but you do have the capacity now to make almost any situation come good.
Love 15, 16. Fortune 21, 22. Health 29, 30. Recharge 7, 8.

FEBRUARY   Seclusion is not something that you would normally seek, and when you do feel insular, others also find the situation difficult to deal with. However, there are quite a few occasions this month when the astrological cycles show that you need time to think. To avoid any difficulties, all you have to do is to explain yourself. Romance could play a part in the latter stages of the month.
Love 13, 14. Fortune 19, 20. Health 27, 28. Recharge 5, 6.

MARCH   Could it be that you are taking life more seriously than the bright and breezy sign of Aquarius is apt to do? Once again you throw up puzzles for others, though this is not to suggest that you find this to be at all a difficult period across the board. Try for changes of scenery, altered ways of looking at things and the possiblity of taking on a little more in the way of responsibility.
Love 13, 14. Fortune 19, 20. Health 27, 28. Recharge 5, 6.

APRIL   A far less repressed Aquarian looks out at April, probably the first month of the year when you show yourself at your very best and most typical. This means that you automatically make a good impression and this in itself acts as a sort of springboard into new incentives, greater financial potential and greater fun. Definitely a time to allow the best of yourself to be on show.
Love 11, 12. Fortune 17, 18. Health 25, 26. Recharge 3, 4.

MAY   May continues your search for popularity, though, as with all astrological cycles, the outcome depends on how you choose to use the trend. A potential love of deep mystery and 'hidden' subjects is also likely to become evident. Perhaps you can find a way to sort out a puzzle from the past and do yourself no end of good as a result. Don't be frightened to enlist friends.
Love 9, 10. Fortune 15, 16. Health 23, 24. Recharge 1, 2.

JUNE   Once June really gets underway you can expect to be facing up to a few home truths, though you should not expect the result of these considerations to be necessarily bad. On the contrary, a better knowledge of what you have been also allows subtle changes to be made. The effect of these may not show within June itself, but can prove to be very far-reaching in the weeks and months ahead.
Love 7, 8. Fortune 13, 14. Health 21, 22. Recharge 29, 30.

JULY   Whatever plans you might have made in advance, there is little doubt that July is potentially the best time of the year for Aquarians who wish to travel. At work you are now showing your true potential, or at least you should do your best to make an impression. The reason is simple, you cannot help standing out from the crowd professionally, and the fact is noticed.
Love 5, 6. Fortune 11, 12. Health 19, 20. Recharge 27, 28.

AQUARIUS BORN PEOPLE

AUGUST   You can climb out of any minor mishaps that life appears to place in your path, but it might be sensible not to allow yourself to fall into them in the first place. This means keeping your wits about you, in the way that no sign can better. Confidence might seem to be difficult to find, but if so take heart. In all probability you make a better impression than you think.
Love 3, 4. Fortune 9, 10. Health 17, 18. Recharge 25, 26.

SEPTEMBER   September turns out to be a month of alternatives, and a time when it is very difficult to take almost anything at face value. Nobody is better than you are at finding something significant, even in the strangest situations. This is a skill that comes into its own so much now that you may even surprise yourself. A bit of cheek would work wonders took, so if you want it, just ask!
Love 1, 2. Fortune 7, 8. Health 15, 16. Recharge 23, 24.

OCTOBER   Many areas of life now seem very normal, and perhaps routine. The fact is that earlier months have been different to say the least, and all that you find yourself surrounded by now is normality. If you don't like this state of affairs, you do have the power to change it. On the other hand, routines do allow you to catch up with situations that have to be dealt with sometime.
Love 30, 31. Fortune 5, 6. Health 13, 14. Recharge 21, 22.

NOVEMBER   Potentially good times romantically now look you in the face. Aquarians who are in established relationships should be making more of them, whilst younger or single Water Carriers can look towards a new start. Socially speaking the chances are that you will find youself in great demand and may have to be very selective about just what you are willing to undertake.
Love 28, 29. Fortune 3, 4. Health 11, 12. Recharge 19, 20.

DECEMBER   December can be a riot of colour and activity, even if it does start out quite slowly. Here we find a path to possible happiness, because you have the time to lay down Christmas plans, deal with family concerns and help out a friend or two. Give yourself up totally to the celebrations that come along later and at the same time don't turn away from personal development.
Love 26, 27. Fortune 1, 2. Health 9, 10. Recharge 17, 18.

PISCES BORN PEOPLE

Birthdays between February 20th and March 20th inclusive. Your planet is Neptune. Birthstone, bloodstone. Lucky day, Thursday.

SUN–MOON CYCLES: All astrology depends on cycles, and at the end of each month in the readings below, you will find a series of diary dates, each connected with the commencement of a two-day cycle that relates to the moving Moon and its association with your Sun sign. The dates listed are headed **Love, Fortune, Health** and **Recharge**. The first three indicate times when effort really pays out in the area concerned, whilst **Recharge** means putting in less effort and taking a break from pressure.

JANUARY   The average Piscean is soft, sensitive and passive, so imagine the surprise of the world at large when it discovers that you begin the year hard, determined and active. Your concern for others remains intact, but there is a good chance that you want to push your own ideas forward too. Don't necessarily accept what life offers if it doesn't agree with what you want.
Love 16, 17. Fortune 23, 24. Health 30, 31. Recharge 9, 10.

PISCES BORN PEOPLE

FEBRUARY Most people will be happy to discover that you are back to normal, though of course this is a relative word when speaking about your very original zodiac sign. Time slows down now, and there should seem to be plenty of it to push in almost any direction that takes your fancy. Don't rush your fences and make the most of all the love and support that is there for the taking.
Love 15, 16. Fortune 21, 22. Health 27, 28. Recharge 7, 8.

MARCH Cause and effect are the lessons for Pisces during March. Situations from the past are almost certain to come back into your life now, and the way that you find yourself dealing with them is all important. The arrival of the Spring should cheer you up no end, and coincides with a fairly long period of greater energy reserves. Allow slower types to keep up with you now.
Love 13, 14. Fortune 19, 20. Health 25, 26. Recharge 5, 6.

APRIL Most Piseceans find this to be a time when they are very much on display. You might not particularly care for the fact, especially if you come from the shy side of your sign. All the same, you can't really lose out by being centre stage and are able to convince others that you know how to get things done. You will respond very well to some changes in scenery later.
Love 11, 12. Fortune 17, 18. Health 23, 24. Recharge 3, 4.

MAY Lovely May brings Pisces out into the open even more. This month can be the repository of some of your most cherished wishes, even if takes effort on your part to bring some of them to fruition. It might seem at first as though confidence is not especially high, even if this is a state of affairs that soon alters. Aspects for love at the end of the month are especially good.
Love 9, 10. Fortune 15, 16. Health 21, 22. Recharge 1, 2.

JUNE June should find you happy and carefree in your general attitude, and in possession of a series of astrological cycles which can have a strong bearing on your working life. At the same time, you shine out and are extremely sociable in your attitude towards friends and strangers alike. More likely to be a month of doing, rather than one of planning. You could be slightly impulsive.
Love 7, 8. Fortune 13, 14. Health 19, 20. Recharge 29, 30.

JULY A real freedom loving Piscean looks out at the world now. So much so in fact that you might not find it possible to tie yourself down as much as certain other individuals would wish you to do. By the middle of the month it is possible that you might be very keen to present a good impression for a host of reasons. Be cautious, because you might not be feeling too responsible.
Love 5, 6. Fortune 11, 12. Health 17, 18. Recharge 27, 28.

AUGUST High flying aspects are now less obvious in the part of the zodiac relating to Pisces. Because of this it is likely that you can expect a quieter month, though there is little doubt that a need for fresh fields and pastures new does remain. This could lead to travel, making August probably the best month of all for many of you to think about taking a long holiday or a short break.
Love 3, 4. Fortune 9, 10. Health 15, 16. Recharge 25, 26.

SEPTEMBER A few minor losses are possible as the month gets started, unless you keep a careful eye on spending and refuse to become involved in the sort of speculation that your sign is not noted for. A nostalgic phase is also likely, and this means that you could be taking too much notice of things that have gone before, whilst Old Moore advises keeping a firm eye on the here and now if possible.
Love 1, 2. Fortune 7, 8. Health 13, 14. Recharge 23, 24.

PISCES BORN PEOPLE

OCTOBER Aspects leading to enterprise and determination are probably not lost on you, at a time when you are once again rising to a challenge in a more dynamic way than Pisces normally would. It seems that you should be riding the wave of success that you are more than capable of creating now. If not everyone has your best interests at heart, at least you can be sure you recognise the fact.
Love 30, 31. Fortune 5, 6. Health 11, 12. Recharge 21, 22.

NOVEMBER November almost certainly leads you back to the quiet and more contemplative qualities of your sign. Many of you will prefer to stay close to home and would not be too keen to take on major challenges or to become involved in situations that are alien to you. As the month advances, you become more susceptible to the flattery that is being directed at you in a romantic sense.
Love 28, 29. Fortune 3, 4. Health 9, 10. Recharge 19, 20.

DECEMBER Nobody is forced by astrology, simply advised. The way that you respond to December is proof of this fact. Everything lines up to see you finishing the year in a stronger position financially, though there are other trends that show a slightly lazy streak. As to which of these tendencies predominate, in the end only each Piscean subject is in a position to decide for themselves.
Love 26, 27. Fortune 1, 2. Health 7, 8. Recharge 17, 18.

ARIES BORN PEOPLE

Birthdays between March 21st and April 20th inclusive. Your planet is Mars. Birthstone, diamond. Lucky day, Tuesday.

SUN–MOON CYCLES: All astrology depends on cycles, and at the end of each month in the readings below, you will find a series of diary dates, each connected with the commencement of a two-day cycle that relates to the moving Moon and its association with your Sun sign. The dates listed are headed **Love, Fortune, Health** and **Recharge**. The first three indicate times when effort really pays out in the area concerned, whilst **Recharge** means putting in less effort and taking a break from pressure.

JANUARY At the very start of the year there can be something of a conflict between the way you like things to be personally, and needs that you know others have of you. You soon get into the swing of things and achieve a sensible balance. Look out later for better financial trends and for the sort of luck which did not come your way during the lasst couple of months or so.
Love 18, 19. Fortune 25, 26. Health 1, 2. Recharge 11, 12.

FEBRUARY It may be necessary to suspend your disbelief on one or two occasions at the start of February. Unusual happenings abound, and the world is likely to see a much more sensitive Aries subject than it usually expects. Creating space to stop and think would be sensible at some stage, but not easy later, at a time when there appears to be so much that you must get done.
Love 16, 17. Fortune 23, 24. Health 28, 29. Recharge 9, 10.

MARCH The goodwill of others is most important now, and particularly so when you are faced with projects that would be difficult to undertake alone. Your communication skills are not quite so well emphasised during March, all the more reason to listen to what otehrs are saying before you react. Plans and projects from the past come good towards the end of March, but keep your eye on the ball.
Love 14, 15. Fortune 23, 24. Health 28, 29. Recharge 9, 10.

ARIES BORN PEOPLE

APRIL   Gradually, but definitely, it becomes obvious that life is putting you in the driving seat, though this trend only works to your advantage if you decide to move the vehicle. April can be very rewarding, or a little disappointing. It really all depends on the way you take life on and make it work for you. Quiet spells are inevitable, and prove to be extremely useful too.
Love 11, 13. Fortune 21, 22. Health 26, 27. Recharge 7, 8.

MAY   You are now a modern, progressive and up to the minute Arian subject, which means you can talk to almost anyone about any number of topics. The fact that astrological trends make you less likely to be embarrassed during May means that you sort out problems that might have been difficult earlier. Hard cash transactions would respond to careful and sensitive handling.
Love 10, 11. Fortune 19, 20. Health 24, 25. Recharge 5, 6.

JUNE   Situations that are difficult should be dealt with immediately at the start of this month, and that way the lighter and brighter trends that come along later will be of much more use to you. Some strange and unusual people have a role to play in your life, and they may bring with them a way of looking at things, especially professional matters, that hasn't occurred to you.
Love 8, 9. Fortune 17, 18. Health 22, 23. Recharge 3, 4.

JULY   You don't need to be brave, it comes as second nature to your sign. Difficult sorts of people won't get anywhere with you now, at a time when you are much more likely to get your own way. Family based trends show that there are gains coming via relatives later in the month, as long as you take time out and are not too busy with the practicalities of life.
Love 6, 7. Fortune 15, 16. Health 20, 21. Recharge 1, 2.

AUGUST   A love of luxury and a desire to please yourself could well act as obstacles during the high summer. If you utilise the aspects causing this trend wisely, you will travel as much as you can, and also join in celebrations that have a positive part to play in your life. On the other hand, you could easily just sit back and allow yourself to be lazy. As always, the choice is yours.
Love 4, 5. Fortune 13, 14. Health 18, 19. Recharge 30, 31.

SEPTEMBER   Things are not always exactly what they seem, a fact that turns out to be more obvious than ever during September. If you prepare yourself for the unexpected, you won't be too surprised when it does come along. You can afford to take some unusual situations on board, because in the fullness of time you learn that life definitely does have your best interests at heart.
Love 2, 3. Fortune 11, 12. Health 16, 17. Recharge 28, 29.

OCTOBER   October is a time when you need to react quickly. Fortunately, this is not at all difficult for you, in fact this sort of behaviour comes as second nature. The more dynamic you are, the better things turn out. In between, you will need to take a little time out for relatives, who are in need of the practical advice that you are able to offer under almost all circumstances.
Love 30, 31. Fortune 9, 10. Health 14, 15. Recharge 26, 27.

NOVEMBER   As the winter comes into sight, so at least a part of your nature wants to hibernate. Of course, with the practicalities of life to be dealt with, this won't be possible. By the end of the second week you are fully in gear again and anxious to make situations work out to your advantage. Routines could prove to be tedious, so do your best to use present trends to ring the changes.
Love 28, 29. Fortune 7, 8. Health 12, 13. Recharge 24, 25.

DECEMBER   This month is so full of celebrations, that there seems to be little or no time to get on with the real aspects of life, that definitely take second place. This could lead to frustration if you spend all month trying to swim against the tide. All the same, there is a middle path, on which you can use happy events as a springboard into possibilities that come along later.
Love 26, 27. Fortune 5, 6. Health 9, 10. Recharge 22, 23.

TAURUS BORN PEOPLE

Birthdays between April 21st and May 21st inclusive. Your planet is Venus. Birthstone, emerald. Lucky day, Friday.

SUN-MOON CYCLES: All astrology depends on cycles, and at the end of each month in the readings below, you will find a series of diary dates, each connected with the commencement of a two-day cycle that relates to the moving Moon and its association with your Sun sign. The dates listed are headed **Love, Fortune, Health** and **Recharge**. The first three indicate times when effort really pays out in the area concerned, whilst **Recharge** means putting in less effort and taking a break from pressure.

JANUARY   Don't try too hard to get everything done at once as soon as the year gets started. As long as you bear in mind that there will be time for everything, then you can't go far wrong. Attitude problems pull you up in your tracks initially, though given time you probably start to adopt a newer and better view of life than has been possible previously. A subtle, though definite, turning point.
Love 19, 20. Fortune 27, 28. Health 5, 6. Recharge 13, 14.

FEBRUARY   The more support you have when it comes to new ideas, the greater is your chance that they will work in your favour. This might mean having to enlist suport, because very little comes to you this month unless you are willing to go out and look for it. Family pressures are dealt with easily and there is every chance that love comes knocking at your door at some stage later.
Love 17, 18. Fortune 25, 26. Health 3, 4. Recharge 11, 12.

MARCH   You need to be certain that professional efforts early in March are really the ones that you have been looking for. Some time out to rest and think would be a help, though might be difficult to find during a period when there is potentially so much to be done. A delicate balancing act is the best course of action, with plenty of support available from friends and family.
Love 17, 18. Fortune 25, 26. Health 3, 4. Recharge 11, 12.

APRIL   April is less demanding, and probably also slightly less interesting. You have to put a great deal in socially if you want the month to be particularly eventful and could easily tire yourself on the way. Unusual happenings are possible, not least of all in your personal life, when attention comes to you from directions that may surprise you. Your standards are high.
Love 15, 16. Fortune 23, 24. Health 1, 2. Recharge 9, 10.

MAY   Be prepared. Confidence is at an all time high, and you need to make the most of the fact from the very first day of the month. Entertainment is self-created, so other people should find you to be fun to have around. You present yourself to the world in the best possible light, and that means that gains come as second nature. A lovely time to be a Taurean, if you make use of the fact.
Love 13, 14. Fortune 21, 22. Health 30, 31. Recharge 7, 8.

JUNE   You are fully aware of your potential, and though you are somewhat quieter than may have been the case last month, now you are able to consolidate. Working alongside others, you discover aspects to people's natures that you hardly suspected. It's important to balance the practical and the fun, though it seems rather unnecessary to overstate a fact you probably already appreciate.
Love 11, 12. Fortune 19, 20. Health 28, 29. Recharge 5, 6.

JULY   Situations that could have moved you in the past are now much more likely to leave you cold. You might be accused of being rather too calculating, and as a result, others may not warm to you as much as usual. The best bet is to allow your softer side to show. This way you will make the most out of yourself for the whole month and can be certain of continuing to make an impression too.
Love 9, 10. Fortune 17, 18. Health 26, 27. Recharge 1, 2.

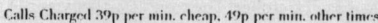
..24..

TAURUS BORN PEOPLE

AUGUST   Certainly a good month for travel, no matter if it is for the sake of a holiday or on account of work. Creating a space for yourself in life is most important, and becomes easier now that you are being watched so closely, and probably admired too. Confidence this month tends to be quite high, though not so much if you step beyond the bounds of what you know and understand.
Love 7, 8. Fortune 15, 16. Health 24, 25. Recharge 1, 2.

SEPTEMBER   Because you are likely to be looking at potentials now, you might also feel slightly more vulnerable. This in itself could lead to a quieter month, which would be a pity at a time when you have so much to offer. Get any small difficulties out of the way as soon as they crop up, leaving yourself more time to pl.ease yourself later on. Later vacations could suit some Taureans, as travel still suits you.
Love 5, 6. Fortune 13, 14. Health 22, 23. Recharge 29, 30.

OCTOBER   Before you can take any sort of action, you need to be in full possession of all the facts. This may not be all that easy on occasions in October. The trouble is that you can be easily misled, if not by people then by situations. Although the month is generally a good one, it would be sensible not to take things at face value, but to test things out for yourself if possible.

NOVEMBER   November brings darker nights, but a lighter feel to life as far as your sign is concerned. Active and enterprising for most of the time, you might see this as a good period for making any sort of necessary changes with regard to work. You seem to be held in high esteem and your Taurean fineness of touch is much in evidence. Definitely a very creative period in the offing.
Love 1, 2. Fortune 9, 10. Health 18, 19. Recharge 25, 26.

DECEMBER   Looking back at the year, you should have good reason to feel that you have come a long way during 1996. Not that the work is over yet. A natural desire to move forward, personally and financially, is endemic to your nature right now. There may be little enough time to think about Christmas, and in any case, many of the really happy times now come of their own accord.
Love 30, 31. Fortune 7, 8. Health 16, 17. Recharge 23, 24.

 # GEMINI BORN PEOPLE

Birthdays between May 22nd and June 21st inclusive. Your planet is Mercury. Birthstone, agate. Lucky day, Wednesday.

SUN–MOON CYCLES: All astrology depends on cycles, and at the end of each month in the readings below, you will find a series of diary dates, each connected with the commencement of a two-day cycle that relates to the moving Moon and its association with your Sun sign. The dates listed are headed **Love, Fortune, Health** and **Recharge**. The first three indicate times when effort really pays out in the area concerned, whilst **Recharge** means putting in less effort and taking a break from pressure.

JANUARY   A typical Gemini is on display at the moment, and there is plenty to occupy you almost from the word go. The main trends this month tend to lead you in the direction of better work prospects and the ability to impress people at all levels. Don't stand aside from this ability and, at the same time, look towards better travel prospects and the ability to make your own choices.
Love 22, 23. Fortune 30, 31. Health 7, 8. Recharge 15, 16.

GEMINI BORN PEOPLE

FEBRUARY   Although it looks as though you will be slightly quieter in some ways during February, you are still good to know and able to make the sort of impression on life that your zodiac sign is famous for. Psychologically speaking you are working your way through past difficulties and sorting them out in your mind. For this reason, progress tends to be slow, but extremely useful all the same.
Love 20, 21. Fortune 28, 29. Health 5, 6. Recharge 13, 14.

MARCH   Genuine Gemini confidence starts to increase now, and there should be plenty going on in your life as the spring starts to show itself. Perhaps you ought to be asking yourself if you are getting the rest that your overworked constitution really needs. A good month for taking new regimes on board and for laying down plans for later in the year, especially ones related to travel.
Love 18, 19. Fortune 26, 27. Health 3, 4. Recharge 11, 12.

APRIL   The best gift in the armoury of life for your sign at the moment is intuition, and you should notice during April that it is the 'undertones' of life that are all important right now. Not that this prevents you from being active and enterprising, though there are many occasions when you can achieve a great deal, and without haviung to flog yourself to death in order to do so.
Love 16, 17. Fortune 24, 25. Health 1, 2. Recharge 9, 10.

MAY   Less impulsive than is sometimes the case, you are presently more likely to be a serious-minded Gemini and well able to weigh up the possibilities in any potential situation. Confidence should be fairly high, and as the Sun moves back towards your birth degree, you should also notice that your general level of good luck is on the increase. Romance is a distinct possibility later on.
Love 14, 15. Fortune 22, 23. Health 30, 31. Recharge 7, 8.

JUNE   Almost anything attracts you during June, except the matter in hand. Your often outrageous behaviour is probably less likely to be shocking to others, so that with a mixture of cheek and personality, you could get away with almost anything. An active phase later in the month would mark a time when travel might be a good thing, as well as the possiblity of making some new friends.
Love 12, 13. Fortune 20, 21. Health 28, 29. Recharge 5, 6.

JULY   Creating a good impression is really not at all difficult, as you are already aware. You might have to work harder this month in other respects however and there is little doubt that the more you slog away, the better things will turn out in the fullness of time. Don't expect rewards to come in thick and fast because they won't, and yet the undertones of life are quite positive.
Love 10, 11. Fortune 18, 19. Health 26, 27. Recharge 3, 4.

AUGUST   Gemini is not against standing up for itself when it proves to be necessary to do so, and you find yourself going through a phase in August when you really do have to tell the world what you are about and what you believe. When under the glare of the public gaze you are almost certain to come good. When routines threaten to get you down, it's time to leave them alone.
Love 8, 9. Fortune 16, 17. Health 24, 25. Recharge 1, 2.

SEPTEMBER   You may not think that you are setting the right example at present but there are plenty of people who will be paying you a great deal of attention. Probably the best month of the year financially, though only if you take note of the way that trends are running and react accordingly. Creating space to do your own thing is important, particularly at the end of the month.
Love 6, 7. Fortune 14, 15. Health 22, 23. Recharge 29, 30.

OCTOBER   Expectations are high at the moment, and if you really put some effort in, you can be fairly certain that life will back you up. Acting on impulse is part of what you are, so that avoiding doing so would be very difficult. A view of your possibilities professionally towards the end of the year makes it possible to start arranging things in a more concrete sense now.
Love 4, 5. Fortune 12, 13. Health 20, 21. Recharge 27, 28.

GEMINI BORN PEOPLE

NOVEMBER: Revelations coming in from outside set the month apart, and might make it appear from time to time that you have little choice in the way things are going. In fact this is almost certainly not true and this is not time to be giving in, just because the going gets tough. Any victory that you manage to achieve during November is particularly welcome because of your own efforts.
Love 2, 3. Fortune 10, 11. Health 18, 18. Recharge 25, 26.

DECEMBER If you are tired with the same old routines, this month does at least give you the chance to ring the changes, and to get to grips with a Christmas period that you can really enjoy. A potentially active time, but one that also demands periods of reflection, something your sign never gets enough of. You can't get enough of interesting people either, and there are many of them around.
Love 29, 30. Fortune 8, 9. Health 16, 17. Recharge 23, 24.

 # CANCER BORN PEOPLE

Birthdays between June 22nd and July 22nd inclusive. Your planet is the Moon. Birthstone, ruby. Lucky day, Monday.

SUN–MOON CYCLES: All astrology depends on cycles, and at the end of each month in the readings below, you will find a series of diary dates, each connected with the commencement of a two-day cycle that relates to the moving Moon and its association with your Sun sign. The dates listed are headed **Love, Fortune, Health** and **Recharge**. The first three indicate times when effort really pays out in the area concerned, whilst **Recharge** means putting in less effort and taking a break from pressure.

JANUARY What you want for yourself at the start of the year, and the demands that other people make of you, can be two entirely different things, so that striking a sensible balance is probably your task for January. Perhaps you are too demanding of yourself, though you can expect to have a good time, especially towards the end of the month, when personal choices are greater.
Love 25, 26. Fortune 4, 5. Health 11, 12. Recharge 17, 18.

FEBRUARY The most important people in your life are the individuals you love personally, and this aspect of your lunar ruled sign has rarely been more evident than it is during February. This might make it difficult for you to turn your mind outwards now, though to try and do so is clearly very important. Look towards possible alterations on the professional front as March approaches.
Love 23, 24. Fortune 2, 3. Health 9, 10. Recharge 15, 16.

MARCH The impact of past events may play the most important part in the way that you are looking at life right now. This can make you rather nostalgic on occasions and too much of this sort of thinking is not good for you. Alternatively, there are many new options in store, like planning for the summer in terms of new professional possibilities and also travel. A time to look ahead.
Love 23, 24. Fortune 2, 3. Health 9, 10. Recharge 15, 16.

APRIL Some very important people should be coming into your life at present, even if you may not exactly recognise the fact at first. Slipping into new routines should come fairly easy now, and achieving an adequate balance between practical requirements and personal needs is also not difficult. Probably not a highly eventful month, but none the less useful if you are sensible.
Love 21, 22. Fortune 29, 30. Health 7, 8. Recharge 13, 14.

MAY Things become generally more interesting, and the nearer the Sun draws to its position at the time of your birth, the better the year works out for you. This leaves you a couple of months to get practical matters sorted out and to lay down plans for the way you want to use the time to come. It is possible to make sensible compromises, especially in personal relationships.
Love 19, 20. Fortune 27, 28. Health 5, 6. Recharge 11, 12.

CANCER BORN PEOPLE

JUNE There are some quite intimidating people around at the moment, not that you will allow them to get in your way. Cancer can be much more dynamic now and you may even surprise one or two people who expect you to constantly take a back seat. Life becomes faster and more exciting as the month passes by, but it is very necessary to give it a slight push from time to time during June.
Love 17, 18. Fortune 25, 26. Health 3, 4. Recharge 9, 10.

JULY Nothing is quite as simple as it first appears and it proves to be possible to make more than one gain out of practically any situation now. Probably the most rewarding month for you, with general luck improved and more influence over your life as a whole. As always, give and take are important, but there are some people about who should make certain you are on the receiving end.
Love 15, 16. Fortune 23, 24. Health 1, 2. Recharge 7, 8.

AUGUST Positive situations have the chance to consolidate in your life, as astrological cycles offer greater personal choice and a greater sense of your own worth. There are things that you find out about yourself now that can have a profound bearing on the way you behave for the rest of the year. Listen to what your inner mind is telling you, because its advice is generally sound.
Love 13, 14. Fortune 21, 22. Health 30, 31. Recharge 5, 6.

SEPTEMBER Once again, and typical of your sign, you turn back to your first love, which is home and family. Any dissatisfaction early in the month is soon dispelled as you commit yourself to family projects and to the need that your friends have of you. A deeply romantic phase is in the offing, and if you are single this could be seen as a time of potential new relationships coming into your life.
Love 11, 12. Fortune 19, 20. Health 28, 29. Recharge 3, 4.

OCTOBER Your self esteem may not be quite as high as it should be, particularly bearing in mind that there are some significant successes in your life during October. Listen to what others are saying about you, because, in the main, they are telling the truth. It won't take you long to feel on top of the world again and the lure of the next horizon could well captivate you.
Love 9, 10. Fortune 17, 18. Health 26, 27. Recharge 1, 2.

NOVEMBER Practical considerations improve, so that there could be either more money about or perhaps a greater ability to make circumstances work out more or less the way you would wish. Astrological cycles now favour advancement, and this strikes as much in your home life as it does at work. Your own profile in the eyes of others is raised significantly, and life should smile on you.
Love 7, 8. Fortune 15, 16. Health 25, 26. Recharge 29, 30.

DECEMBER December is likely to be quiet at its start, though it does speed up considerably as you approach the Christmas period. Keep faith with your ideas and your efforts because they prove to be very important to you. The more joy you can bring into the lives of those around you, the better the period turns out to be for you too. Some crucial decisions are made towards the end of the year.
Love 5, 6. Fortune 13, 14. Health 23, 24. Recharge 27, 28.

.. 32 ..

LEO BORN PEOPLE

Birthdays between July 23rd and August 23rd inclusive. Your planet is the Sun. Birthstone, sapphire. Lucky day, Sunday.

SUN–MOON CYCLES: All astrology depends on cycles, and at the end of each month in the readings below, you will find a series of diary dates, each connected with the commencement of a two-day cycle that relates to the moving Moon and its association with your Sun sign. The dates listed are headed **Love, Fortune, Health** and **Recharge**. The first three indicate times when effort really pays out in the area concerned, whilst **Recharge** means putting in less effort and taking a break from pressure.

JANUARY   Start out as you mean to go on, bold Leo. The more effort you put in at the beginning of January, the better things are likely to go for you in a practical sense later on. In an effort to spread the load slightly, you can make use of the very real help that is on offer from other people. The best cycles of all relate to your ability to make more money and to get on top of past problems.
Love 30, 31. Fortune 6, 7. Health 14, 15. Recharge 21, 22.

FEBRUARY   February brings slight reversals, and the way that you deal with these is all important. People expect to see the bright and cheerful side of your nature, and even when your appearance is little more than a sham, it can still have the same end result. The winter could get you down a little and it's really a case of keeping summer in your heart, despite the state of the weather outside.
Love 28, 29. Fortune 4, 5. Health 12, 13. Recharge 19, 20.

MARCH   Learn to sit back and watch life for a change, instead of constantly trying to make things work out as you would wish. There are strong trends around to indicate that most situations turn out well for you in the end, so wasting energy would be a mistake. Love and romance come your way in March, together with a feeling that you are making greater progress in your professional endeavours.
Love 28, 29. Fortune 4, 5. Health 12, 13. Recharge 19, 20.

APRIL   Upheavals in the family at the start of the month are unlikely to last all that long; all the more reason to dismiss them from your mind and to get on with the many practical requirements that are demanding your attention. Your executive skills are well accented and you want to do all you can to build on naturally good trends financially. Stay in the good books of all family members.
Love 26, 27. Fortune 2, 3. Health 10, 11. Recharge 17, 18.

MAY   May brings a slow start, a busy middle and a slightly confusing conclusion. All of this is a little irrelevant however, since you are now well able to deal with most situations, as and when they occur. It's time to chase a dream to its logical conclusion, and there is plenty of help and support to do so. A new and interesting creative trend is there for the taking.
Love 24, 25. Fortune 30, 31. Health 8, 9. Recharge 15, 16.

JUNE   The great and the good are likely to be crossing your path now, and you could do much worse than to latch onto a winning combination of the aspects that sit around your sign at present. You are good to be with, happy to ring the changes for the sake of others, and willing to show just what Leo is capable of at its best. Leo is always the king of the zodiac signs, but never more so than now.
Love 22, 23. Fortune 28, 29. Health 6, 7. Recharge 13, 14.

JULY   A happy time is likely, even if one or two personal frustrations are difficult to deal with. When problems do arise, untypically, you are likely to hide them away, which may not be the best course of action. Financially speaking, things can go your way, though not unless you put yourself in the right position to gain from them. Beware a slightly ruthless streak later in the month, and control it.
Love 20, 21. Fortune 26, 27. Health 4, 5. Recharge 11, 12.

                                                      Cont'd on p.48

JANUARY

For High Water add, for Bristol 5h. 30m., Hull 4h. 23m., Leith 0h. 43m., and for Dublin sub. 2h. 21m., Greenock 1h. 26m., Liverpool 2h. 29m.

D of M	D of W	Sundays, Festivals Special Events, etc., for 1996	Sun Rises R Sets S	High Water at London Bridge		Moon at London		Wea-ther
				Morn.	After.	Rises	Sets	
			h. m.	h. m.	h. m.	h. m.	h. m.	
1	M	New Year's Day	R 8 06	10 15	22 59	13 20	3 46	
2	Tu	Bank Holiday (Scot.)	S16 02	11 27	23 59	13 57	4 46	
3	W	Lord Haw-Haw hanged 1946	R 8 06	—	12 23	14 38	5 41	
4	Th	Utah 45th US state 1896	S16 04	0 47	13 08	15 26	6 31	with
5	F	X-rays demonstrated 1896	R 8 05	1 26	13 46	16 19	7 15	winter
6	S	Epiphany/Twelfth Night	S16 07	2 02	14 21	17 16	7 53	of
7	☙	1st Sunday after Epiphany	R 8 04	2 35	14 55	18 16	8 27	spell
8	M	Plough Monday	S16 09	3 08	15 29	19 19	8 56	coldest
9	Tu	Lord Nelson buried 1806	R 8 03	3 41	16 04	20 23	9 22	the
10	W	First UN assembly 1946	S16 12	4 14	16 38	21 28	9 46	expect spells.
11	Th	King Zog deposed 1946	R 8 02	4 48	17 13	22 34	10 09	can bright
12	F	J. Pestalozzi b. 1746	S16 15	5 20	17 49	23 42	10 33	we intermittent
13	S	Glencoe massacre 1692	R 8 01	5 55	18 30	—	10 58	month be
14	☙	2nd Sunday after Epiphany	S16 18	6 39	19 22	0 52	11 26	the will
15	M	Aristotle Onassis b. 1906	R 8 00	7 38	20 31	2 04	11 59	of there
16	Tu	Diana Wynyard b. 1906	S16 21	8 59	21 51	3 16	12 40	half but
17	W	St Anthony of Egypt	R 7 58	10 22	23 04	4 27	13 29	first –
18	Th	Rudyard Kipling d. 1936	S16 24	11 35	—	5 33	14 30	the snowfalls
19	F	Dolly Parton b. 1946	R 7 56	0 11	12 40	6 30	15 40	During periodic
20	S	George Burns b. 1896	S16 27	1 08	13 35	7 19	16 57	
21	☙	3rd Sunday after Epiphany	R 7 54	1 57	14 24	7 59	18 18	
22	M	1st day of Ramadan	S16 31	2 45	15 12	8 33	19 38	
23	Tu	Shensi earthquake 1556	R 7 52	3 30	15 58	9 03	20 56	
24	W	Conscription introd. 1916	S16 34	4 14	16 43	9 30	22 11	
25	Th	Burns Night	R 7 49	4 56	17 27	9 57	23 22	
26	F	Australia Day	S16 38	5 40	18 11	10 23	—	
27	S	*Apollo 1* fire tragedy 1967	R 7 47	6 23	18 57	10 52	0 31	
28	☙	4th Sunday after Epiphany	S16 41	7 11	19 49	11 23	1 36	
29	M	Sacha Distel b. 1933	R 7 44	8 10	20 51	11 58	2 38	
30	Tu	Hallé Orchestra f'd 1858	S16 45	9 22	22 10	12 38	3 35	
31	W	A.A. Milne d. 1956	R 7 41	10 52	23 27	13 23	4 27	

MOON'S PHASES JANUARY 1996		Days	Hrs.	Mins.
○	Full Moon	5	20	51
☾	Last Quarter	13	20	45
●	New Moon	20	12	50
☽	First Quarter	27	11	14

All times on this page are GMT

PREDICTIONS

The Full Moon on the 5th is in Cancer and falls in the eleventh house at Westminster, highlighting parliamentary matters, and the government will be successfully obtaining approval for a foreign treaty, probably involving fisheries. *Mars is conjunct Neptune and Uranus,* raising a risk of oil and gas leaks, a major scandal, minor earth tremors and random terrorist attacks. Globally California and the Gulf are the two areas highlighted. Russia enters the year in a state of military and economic disruption, and the beginning of the month could bring a military coup. There is a great danger of instability elsewhere in the same region, and the West may threaten sanctions against some repressive states.

The New Moon on the 20th falls in Capricorn and is in the ninth house at Westminster, raising constitutional questions concerning Parliament's ability to control the government. In the Balkans, Serbia will be at the forefront of peace moves, initiating a new agreement. There is likely to be civil strife in Macedonia. There will be extravagant proposals in the European Union for a single currency and expansion. These are unlikely to be accepted.

Favourites may be worth following at National Hunt Meetings.

Predicted German Reunification 1990

FRIENDSHIP?

Communism RUSSIA

REPUBLIC ?

FEBRUARY

For High Water add, for Bristol 5h. 30m., Hull 4h. 23m., Leith 0h. 43m., and for Dublin sub. 2h. 21m., Greenock 1h. 26m., Liverpool 2h. 29m.

D of M	D of W	Sundays, Festivals Special Events, etc., for 1996	Sun Rises R Sets S	High Water at London Bridge Morn.	High Water at London Bridge After.	Moon at London Rises	Moon at London Sets	Wea-ther
			h. m.	h. m.	h. m.	h. m.	h. m.	
1	Th	*La Bohème* opened 1896	S16 48	11 58	—	14 14	5 13	
2	F	Candlemas	R 7 38	0 20	12 46	15 09	5 53	
3	S	*Luna IX* moon land'g 1966	S16 52	1 04	13 26	16 08	6 28	
4	☽	Septuagesima Sunday	R 7 35	1 41	14 02	17 10	6 59	
5	M	George Arliss d. 1946	S16 55	2 14	14 35	18 14	7 27	
6	Tu	St Dorothy	R 7 31	2 48	15 08	19 19	7 52	
7	W	Sir Thos More b. 1478	S16 59	3 22	15 43	20 25	8 16	
8	Th	Beatles arr. in NY 1964	R 7 28	3 54	16 15	21 33	8 39	
9	F	Soap rationing began 1942	S17 03	4 25	16 49	22 41	9 04	
10	S	Sophie Tucker d. 1966	R 7 25	4 57	17 23	23 51	9 31	
11	☽	Sexagesima Sunday	S17 06	5 31	18 02	—	10 02	
12	M	James II fled 1688	R 7 21	6 13	18 49	1 01	10 38	
13	Tu	Cath. Howard execut. 1542	S17 10	7 08	19 53	2 10	11 21	
14	W	St Valentine's Day	R 7 17	8 28	21 16	3 16	12 15	
15	Th	George VI's funeral 1952	S17 14	9 57	22 39	4 15	13 18	
16	F	John Schlessinger b. 1926	R 7 13	11 20	23 54	5 07	14 29	
17	S	Marian Anderson b. 1902	S17 17	—	12 27	5 50	15 47	
18	☽	Quinquagesima Sunday	R 7 10	0 53	13 24	6 28	17 06	
19	M	Prince Andrew b. 1960	S17 21	1 45	14 13	7 00	18 26	
20	Tu	Shrove Tuesday	R 7 06	2 30	14 58	7 29	19 44	
21	W	Ash Wednesday	S17 25	3 12	15 40	7 57	20 59	
22	Th	Duchess of Kent b. 1933	R 7 02	3 53	16 21	8 24	22 11	
23	F	L.S. Lowry d. 1976	S17 28	4 34	17 00	8 53	23 20	
24	S	K. Nkrumah exiled 1966	R 6 57	5 11	17 38	9 23	—	
25	☽	1st Sunday in Lent	S17 32	5 51	18 18	9 57	0 25	
26	M	'Buffalo Bill' b. 1846	R 6 53	6 34	19 03	10 36	1 25	
27	Tu	Reichstag fire 1933	S17 35	7 28	20 00	11 19	2 19	
28	W	Moorgate disaster 1975	R 6 49	8 35	21 09	12 08	3 08	
29	Th	Joss Ackland b. 1928	S17 39	10 00	22 39	13 02	3 51	

(Weather column, spanning the month): After then conditions will improve. The period 9th–16th will be extremely cold. After that chilly days. There will be quite a few sunny but chilly days.

MOON'S PHASES FEBRUARY 1996

		Days	Hrs.	Mins.
○	Full Moon	4	15	58
☾	Last Quarter	12	8	37
●	New Moon	18	23	30
☽	First Quarter	26	5	52

All times on this page are GMT

PREDICTIONS

The Full Moon on the 4th is in Leo, and is in the first house at Westminster, indicating pressure for 'popular democracy' but also antagonism in foreign policy. The government will take an aggressively nationalist attitude. However, it is likely to present itself as a friend of Europe, favouring the idea of national independence and opposing federalism. There will be steps to expand the duties of the National Health Service. In Russia there are now signs of nostalgia for the old communist system, and a return of communists to government. The USA will be in action, probably against a dictatorial regime. This falls in line with a more determined American resolution not to allow her interests to be threatened. *The New Moon on the 18th is in Aquarius and falls in the fourth house at London. It is opposed the 'royal star', Regulus,* implying opposition to the monarchy, and the restriction of royal powers. The creation of a republic, will be high up the political agenda. Elections in Macedonia could calm a tense situation. The Japanese economy enters a period of uncertainty. In India there is a risk of a state breaking away, and of war with Pakistan. The Tote Gold Trophy at Newbury may be won by a horse carrying 10 st 9 lbs.

Your LUCKY LOTTERY NUMBERS on page 64

Predicted the abdication of of King Edward VIII 1936

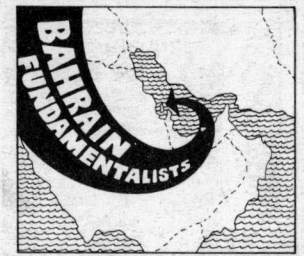

MARCH

For High Water add, for Bristol 5h. 30m., Hull 4h. 23m., Leith 0h. 43m., and for Dublin sub. 2h. 21m., Greenock 1h. 26m., Liverpool 2h. 29m.

D of M	D of W	Sundays, Festivals Special Events, etc., for 1996	Sun Rises R Sets S	High Water at London Bridge Morn.	High Water at London Bridge After.	Moon at London Rises	Moon at London Sets	Weather
			h. m.	h. m.	h. m.	h. m.	h. m.	
1	F	St David	R 6 45	11 27	23 49	13 59	4 28	
2	S	Rhodesia a republic 1970	S17 43	—	12 19	15 00	5 00	
3	☉	2nd Sunday in Lent	R 6 40	0 36	13 00	16 03	5 29	
4	M	Forth rail. bridge op. 1890	S17 46	1 14	13 35	17 08	5 55	
5	Tu	Joseph Stalin d. 1953	R 6 36	1 49	14 09	18 15	6 20	
6	W	Aspirin patent 1899	S17 50	2 23	14 42	19 23	6 44	
7	Th	Stevie Smith d. 1971	R 6 32	2 56	15 18	20 32	7 09	
8	F	St John of God	S17 53	3 30	15 51	21 42	7 36	
9	S	Yuri Gagarin b. 1934	R 6 27	4 03	16 25	22 52	8 06	
10	☉	3rd Sunday in Lent	S17 56	4 36	17 00		8 40	
11	M	Commonwealth Day	R 6 23	5 14	17 40	0 01	9 21	
12	Tu	Liza Minelli b. 1946	S18 00	5 58	18 26	1 07	10 10	
13	W	Joseph Priestly b. 1733	R 6 18	6 54	19 29	2 07	11 07	
14	Th	Jasper Carrott b. 1946	S18 03	8 13	20 51	2 59	12 13	
15	F	Jul. Caesar murder 44 BC	R 6 14	9 41	22 17	3 45	13 26	
16	S	Jerry Lewis b. 1926	S18 07	11 04	23 35	4 23	14 42	
17	☉	Mothering Sunday	R 6 09	—	12 13	4 57	16 00	
18	M	Bank Holiday for NI	S18 10	0 36	13 08	5 27	17 17	
19	Tu	Adolf Eichmann b. 1906	R 6 05	1 28	13 56	5 55	18 33	
20	W	Vernal equinox 08h 03m	S18 14	2 11	14 40	6 22	19 47	
21	Th	Pocahontas d. 1617	R 6 00	2 52	15 19	6 51	20 59	
22	F	Thomas Hughes d. 1896	S18 17	3 32	15 56	7 21	22 07	
23	S	Pakistan a republic 1956	R 5 55	4 08	16 32	7 54	23 10	
24	☉	Passion Sunday	S18 20	4 45	17 06	8 32	—	
25	M	The Annunciation	R 5 51	5 21	17 41	9 14	0 08	
26	Tu	Kyung-Wha Chung b. 1948	S18 24	6 02	18 20	10 01	1 00	
27	W	US Navy created 1794	R 5 46	6 51	19 11	10 53	1 46	
28	Th	Battle of Matapan 1941	S18 27	7 53	20 17	11 49	2 25	
29	F	Royal Albert Hall op. 1871	R 5 42	9 08	21 37	12 48	2 59	
30	S	Francisco de Goya b. 1746	S18 30	10 34	23 02	13 50	3 29	
31	☉	Palm Sunday	R 5 37	11 40	23 58	14 54	3 57	

Weather column (spanning rows): Very changeable, with a cold beginning and occasional snow showers, followed by strong winds and heavy rain. But the month ends with a touch of spring.

PREDICTIONS

The Full Moon on the 5th is in Virgo and falls in the fifth house at Westminster, in opposition to Mars. The Commons — and the country — will be preoccupied with measures to control child abuse and violence against women, and increase female representation in Parliament. The question of women priests will also be on the agenda again, probably with the prospect of the first Anglican female bishop. There could be elections in Bosnia. In Russia a build up of pressure could bring a change of government. Earthquakes could rock parts of Asia around the 5th or 6th of the month and create a threatened repeat of an earlier tragedy.

The New Moon on the 19th is in Pisces, is conjunct Saturn and in the tenth house at Westminster. This is the worst possible news for the government, indicating that even its best thought out ventures will sink without trace. There are likely to be international conflicts involving fish or oil, perhaps a new outbreak of violence between European Union fishermen. There will be trouble with shipping. In Bahrain the fundamentalist threat is now at a peak, with serious strategic problems for the west.

The Lincoln Handicap may be won by a horse carrying 8 st 10 lbs and the Grand National by the favourite.

MOON'S PHASES MARCH 1996			Days	Hrs	Mins
	○	Full Moon	5	9	23
	☾	Last Quarter	12	17	15
	●	New Moon	19	10	45
	☽	First Quarter	27	1	31

All times GMT (BST from March 31 + 1 hour)

Clocks forward, 1 hour 31 March

Total Eclipse of the Moon begins April 3 at 22h.22m, ends April 4 at 01h.58m.

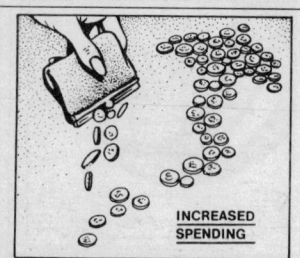

INCREASED SPENDING

HOLY

WARS

Scandal

APRIL

For High Water add, for Bristol 5h. 30m., Hull 4h. 23m., Leith 0h. 43m., and for Dublin sub. 2h. 21m., Greenock 1h. 26m., Liverpool 2h. 29m.

D of M	D of W	Sundays, Festivals Special Events, etc., for 1996	Sun Rises R Sets S	High Water at London Bridge Morn.	High Water at London Bridge After.	Moon at London Rises	Moon at London Sets	Weather
			h. m.	h. m.	h. m.	h. m.	h. m.	
1	M	All Fools' Day	S18 34	—	12 25	16 00	4 22	
2	Tu	Falkland Is invasion 1982	R 5 33	0 40	13 03	17 08	4 47	
3	W	Jesse James shot 1882	S18 37	1 17	13 38	18 17	5 12	
4	Th	1st day of Passover	R 5 28	1 53	14 14	19 28	5 38	
5	F	Good Friday	S18 40	2 28	14 49	20 40	6 07	
6	S	Revd Ian Paisley b. 1926	R 5 24	3 04	15 26	21 51	6 40	
7	☙	Easter Day	S18 44	3 40	16 03	22 59	7 20	
8	M	Easter Monday	R 5 19	4 19	16 42	—	8 07	
9	Tu	Paul Robeson d. 1976	S18 47	5 02	17 24	0 02	9 02	
10	W	Safety pin patented 1849	R 5 15	5 51	18 13	0 57	10 06	
11	Th	Treaty of Utrecht 1713	S18 50	6 51	19 17	1 44	11 15	
12	F	Gargarin earth orbit 1961	R 5 10	8 06	20 34	2 23	12 29	
13	S	Samuel Beckett b. 1906	S18 54	9 26	21 54	2 57	13 44	
14	☙	Low Sunday	R 5 06	10 46	23 13	3 28	14 59	
15	M	The Titanic sank 1912	S18 57	11 54	—	3 55	16 14	
16	Tu	Battle of Culloden 1746	R 5 02	0 16	12 50	4 23	17 27	
17	W	Clare Francis b. 1946	S19 00	1 08	13 36	4 50	18 39	
18	Th	Hayley Mills b. 1946	R 4 58	1 52	14 19	5 19	19 48	
19	F	Pierre Curie d. 1906	S19 04	2 31	14 55	5 51	20 54	
20	S	BBC2 b'n transmit. 1964	R 4 53	3 09	15 30	6 27	21 56	
21	☙	2nd Sunday after Easter	S19 07	3 44	16 04	7 07	22 51	
22	M	Yehudi Menuhin b. 1916	R 4 49	4 19	16 35	7 52	23 40	
23	Tu	St George's Day	S19 10	4 55	17 09	8 43	—	
24	W	Duch. of Windsor d. 1986	R 4 45	5 34	17 45	9 37	0 22	
25	Th	Sir Carol Reed d. 1976	S19 14	6 19	18 30	10 35	0 58	
26	F	Chernobyl explosion 1986	R 4 41	7 12	19 26	11 36	1 30	
27	S	Regent's Park op. 1828	S19 17	8 19	20 41	12 38	1 58	
28	☙	3rd Sunday after Easter	R 4 37	9 32	21 58	13 43	2 23	
29	M	D. of Wellington b. 1769	S19 20	10 41	23 04	14 49	2 48	
30	Tu	A.E. Housman d. 1936	R 4 33	11 37	23 56	15 58	3 12	

Weather column (spanning vertically): A bright start will be followed by occasional snow flurries. It will become warmer mid-month, creating the odd thundery outbreak during the last few days.

PREDICTIONS

The Full Moon on the 4th is an eclipse in Libra. It falls on the midheaven at Westminster and is squared to Jupiter. The government will be excessively confident, and is likely to generate needless battles of principle and destructive muddles, through being cavalier with the people's wishes. There is a strong chance of increased public expenditure and new and unpopular taxes. Internationally there will be a feeling that one must fight for one's beliefs. Any military disputes are therefore likely to be in the nature of crusades, or holy wars. There could be further peace moves in Bosnia.

The New Moon on the 17th is a solar eclipse in Aries, and falls in the fourth house at Westminster. The government will be afflicted by scandal and probably a large financial loss due to a speculative mess, perhaps a currency crisis. Education spending will be increasing, with new measures for nursery provision. The royal family's position is strengthened. The pressure in Russia continues, with possible civil violence, an increase in public mortality, religious and consitutional difficulties.

At Newbury the Greenham Stakes may be won by the favourite, and at Newmarket the Craven Stakes may be won by the second favourite.

MOON'S PHASES APRIL 1996

		Days	Hrs	Mins
○	Full Moon	4	0	7
☽	Last Quarter	10	23	36
●	New Moon	17	22	49
☾	First Quarter	25	20	40

All times on this page are GMT (Add 1 hour BST)

THE OLDEST ANNUAL PUBLICATION

OLD MOORE predicted the General Strike to the day — 3rd May 1926

MAY

For High Water add, for Bristol 5h. 30m., Hull 4h. 23m., Leith 0h. 43m., and for Dublin sub. 2h. 21m., Greenock 1h. 26m., Liverpool 2h. 29m.

D of M	D of W	Sundays, Festivals Special Events, etc., for 1996	Sun Rises R Sets S	High Water at London Bridge Morn.	After.	Moon at London Rises	Sets
			h. m.	h. m.	h. m.	h. m.	h. m.
1	W	Joanna Lumley b. 1946	S19 24	—	12 23	17 08	3 38
2	Th	*Titanic* inquiry op. 1912	R 4 30	0 40	13 05	18 21	4 06
3	F	Eng. Humperdinck b. 1936	S19 27	1 21	13 45	19 34	4 37
4	S	*Daily Mail* publ'd 1896	R 4 26	2 02	14 26	20 46	5 15
5	☀	4th Sunday after Easter	S19 30	2 42	15 05	21 53	6 00
6	M	Bank Holiday	R 4 22	3 23	15 46	22 52	6 54
7	Tu	Eva Perón b. 1919	S19 33	4 08	16 29	23 43	7 56
8	W	Jack Charlton b. 1936	R 4 19	4 56	17 16	—	9 05
9	Th	Glenda Jackson b. 1936	S19 37	5 48	18 08	0 25	10 19
10	F	Maureen Lipman b. 1946	R 4 16	6 49	19 08	1 01	11 33
11	S	Phil Silvers b. 1912	S19 40	7 55	20 16	1 32	12 48
12	☀	Rogation Sunday	R 4 12	9 06	21 29	2 00	14 02
13	M	Tim Pigott-Smith b. 1946	S19 43	10 21	22 46	2 26	15 14
14	Tu	Viscount Allenby d. 1936	R 4 09	11 30	23 52	2 53	16 25
15	W	Ralph Steadman b. 1936	S19 46	—	12 26	3 20	17 34
16	Th	Ascension Day	R 4 06	0 46	13 14	3 50	18 41
17	F	Mafeking relieved 1900	S19 49	1 31	13 56	4 24	19 44
18	S	Gustav Mahler d. 1911	R 4 04	2 11	14 33	5 02	20 42
19	☀	Ascension Sunday	S19 52	2 48	15 06	5 45	21 34
20	M	First H-bomb test 1956	R 4 01	3 23	15 39	6 33	22 19
21	Tu	Daylight saving time int. 1916	S19 54	3 57	16 10	7 27	22 57
22	W	George Best b. 1946	R 3 58	4 34	16 43	8 23	23 31
23	Th	Henrik Ibsen d. 1906	S19 57	5 11	17 20	9 23	—
24	F	Feast of Weeks	R 3 56	5 52	17 59	10 24	0 00
25	S	Bank Holiday Act 1871	S20 00	6 37	18 44	11 27	0 26
26	☀	Whit Sunday/Pentecost	R 3 54	7 29	19 39	12 32	0 51
27	M	Bank Holiday	S20 02	8 33	20 52	13 38	1 14
28	Tu	Dame Thora Hird b. 1916	R 3 52	9 40	22 04	14 47	1 39
29	W	Oak Apple Day	S20 05	10 43	23 06	15 57	2 05
30	Th	P.C. Fabergé b. 1846	R 3 50	11 41	—	17 10	2 34
31	F	Battle of Jutland 1916	S20 07	0 02	12 32	18 24	3 08

Weather: After a chilly start temperatures will rise and there will be a good deal of sunshine during the second week. From about the 18th, expect a mini-heatwave.

MOON'S PHASES MAY 1996

		Days	Hrs	Mins
○	Full Moon	3	11	48
☾	Last Quarter	10	5	4
●	New Moon	17	11	46
☽	First Quarter	25	14	13

All times on this page are GMT (Add 1 hour BST)

PREDICTIONS

The Full Moon on the 3rd is in Scorpio and falls on the IC at Westminster. This is generally favourable for the government, which may expect to make smaller losses than usual at the local elections. Germany will be taking steps to becoming the long-term dominant power in Europe, setting the agenda for increased federalism. Public option is very volatile in the US, and the primaries will give conflicting pictures of the likely Presidential candidates. In Russia, authoritarian rule is favoured, and once again the gaze of the world is on the region, as parties very similar to the old communist model emerge.

The New Moon on the 17th is in Taurus, trine to Neptune. This is bad news for all incumbent politicians who are fighting elections, as contests fought now could involve substantial losses. In addition, decisions taken are unlikely to be lasting, and could be overturned in June. The Prince of Wales' personal life will be under scrutiny. He is coming to the first important set of decisions since his separation, and will seek to formalise his position. If his divorce is not complete he will be seeking to make it so, and could be considering remarriage.

At Newmarket the 2000 Guineas may be won by the favourite, and the 1000 Guineas by a French-trained filly.

says the GUINNESS BOOK OF RECORDS

Predicted Labour Party Re-organisation, June 1994

JUNE

For High Water add, for Bristol 5h. 30m., Hull 4h. 23m., Leith 0h. 43m., and for Dublin sub. 2h. 21m., Greenock 1h. 26m., Liverpool 2h. 29m.

D of M	D of W	Sundays, Festivals Special Events, etc., for 1996	Sun Rises R Sets S	High Water at London Bridge Morn.	High Water at London Bridge After.	Moon at London Rises	Moon at London Sets	Wea-ther
			h. m.	h. m.	h. m.	h. m.	h. m.	
1	S	TV licences issued 1946	R 3 48	0 51	13 19	19 35	3 49	
2	☽	Trinity Sunday	S20 09	1 39	14 04	20 40	4 40	
3	M	Suzi Quatro b. 1946	R 3 47	2 24	14 48	21 36	5 40	
4	Tu	'Suffragette' Derby 1913	S20 11	3 11	15 33	22 24	6 49	
5	W	Lord Kitchener d. 1916	R 3 46	4 00	16 19	23 03	8 03	
6	Th	Corpus Christi	S20 13	4 49	17 09	23 36	9 20	
7	F	Imre Nagy b. 1896	R 3 45	5 41	17 58	—	10 37	
8	S	George Sand d 1876	S20 15	6 36	18 53	0 05	11 52	
9	☽	1st Sunday after Trinity	R 3 44	7 35	19 52	0 32	13 05	
10	M	Prince Philip b. 1921	S20 16	8 38	20 58	0 58	14 16	
11	Tu	Lynsey de Paul b. 1950	R 3 43	9 49	22 14	1 25	15 25	
12	W	Anne Frank b. 1929	S20 17	11 00	23 24	1 54	16 32	
13	Th	Benny Goodman d. 1986	R 3 42	—	12 01	2 25	17 35	
14	F	J. Logie Baird d. 1946	S20 19	0 23	12 51	3 01	18 35	
15	S	Magna Carta signed 1215	R 3 42	1 11	13 35	3 41	19 29	
16	☽	2nd Sunday after Trinity	S20 19	1 52	14 11	4 27	20 16	
17	M	Barry Manilow b. 1946	R 3 42	2 30	14 47	5 19	20 57	
18	Tu	Waterloo Bridge op. 1817	S20 20	3 05	15 18	6 14	21 33	
19	W	Duch. of Windsor b. 1896	R 3 42	3 39	15 50	7 13	22 03	
20	Th	Catherine Cookson b. 1906	S20 21	4 14	16 24	8 13	22 31	
21	F	Summer solstice 02h 24m	R 3 43	4 50	16 59	9 15	22 55	
22	S	Walter de la Mare d. 1956	S20 21	5 27	17 34	10 18	23 19	
23	☽	3rd Sunday after Trinity	R 3 43	6 05	18 12	11 23	23 42	
24	M	W.H. Smith b. 1825	S20 21	6 47	18 54	12 29	—	
25	Tu	Custer's last stand 1876	R 3 44	7 38	19 50	13 37	0 07	
26	W	AA estab. in Britain 1905	S20 21	8 42	21 06	14 47	0 33	
27	Th	Charles Parnell b. 1846	R 3 45	9 54	22 19	15 59	1 04	
28	F	Seychelles independ. 1976	S20 21	11 02	23 27	17 11	1 40	
29	S	Barclaycard introd. 1966	R 3 46	—	12 02	18 19	2 25	
30	☽	4th Sunday after Trinity	S20 21	0 27	12 57	19 21	3 20	

Of late, temperatures for 'Flaming June' have been below average and 1996 is no exception. But they will improve and the last ten days will be warm and sunny.

PREDICTIONS

The Full Moon on the 1st is in Sagittarius and falls in the twelfth house at Westminster, indicating the possibility of prison break outs. A British film or theatrical production could be breaking box office records. Internationally the focus will be on the Balkans, where Albania and Macedonia are under great pressure. Albania is entering a deep crisis while Macedonia could be about to tear itself apart. Greece will be entering a period of national pride, inclining it to see threats where none exist, and it may intervene militarily in Macedonia. The US army will be in action. Egypt takes an unconventional new look at an old problem, and may solve it once and for all.

The New Moon on the 16th is in Gemini, and falls in the second house at Westminster. Matters of war and peace will be at the top of the international agenda, with a major initiative perhaps a conference. The Balkans, especially Macedonia, is the focal point. The position in China looks increasingly unstable, and there is now a chance of a renewed democracy movement. Nationalism is still on the rise in Russia. There is further tension and threat of war in India. The Epsom Derby may be won by the second favourite and the Oaks by the favourite.

MOON'S PHASES JUNE 1996

		Days	Hrs	Mins
○	Full Moon	1	20	47
☾	Last Quarter	8	11	6
●	New Moon	16	1	36
☽	First Quarter	24	5	5

All times on this page are GMT (Add 1 hour BST)

Published EVERY YEAR since 1697

Predicted World War II, 1939

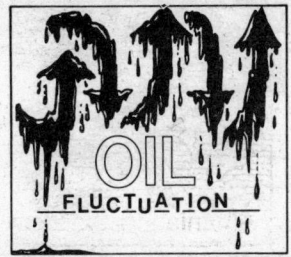
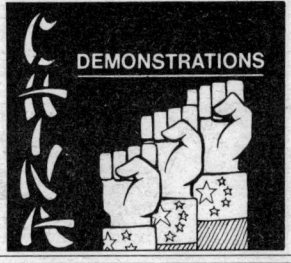

JULY

For High Water add, for Bristol 5h. 30m., Hull 4h. 23m., Leith 0h. 43m., and for Dublin sub. 2h. 21m., Greenock 1h. 26m., Liverpool 2h. 29m.

D of M	D of W	Sundays, Festivals Special Events, etc., for 1996	Sun Rises R Sets S	High Water at London Bridge Morn.	High Water at London Bridge After.	Moon at London Rises	Moon at London Sets	Weather
			h. m.	h. m.	h. m.	h. m.	h. m.	
1	M	H. Beecher Stowe d. 1896	R 3 47	1 22	13 48	20 15	4 25	July sees perfect summer weather with the warmest long spell of the year. There will be a great deal of sunshine and it will be very hot at times.
2	Tu	Kenneth Clarke b. 1940	S20 20	2 11	14 35	20 59	5 39	
3	W	Entebbe Airport raid 1976	R 3 49	3 01	15 22	21 36	6 57	
4	Th	US Independence Day	S20 19	3 50	16 08	22 08	8 17	
5	F	Tom Mboya Assass. 1969	R 3 50	4 38	16 55	22 37	9 35	
6	S	Malawi became repub. 1966	S20 18	5 27	17 42	23 04	10 52	
7	☙	5th Sunday after Trinity	R 3 52	6 16	18 30	23 31	12 05	
8	M	NSPCC founded 1884	S20 17	7 08	19 22	23 59	13 16	
9	Tu	Sir Edward Heath b. 1916	R 3 54	8 04	20 23	—	14 24	
10	W	Sveso poison cloud 1976	S20 15	9 09	21 34	0 29	15 28	
11	Th	John Stride b. 1936	R 3 56	10 24	22 55	1 03	16 29	
12	F	Bank Holiday for NI	S20 13	11 33	23 59	1 41	17 24	
13	S	Titus Oates d. 1705	R 3 58	—	12 27	2 25	18 14	
14	☙	6th Sunday after Trinity	S20 12	0 51	13 12	3 14	18 57	
15	M	St Swithun's Day	R 4 01	1 34	13 52	4 08	19 35	
16	Tu	Mary Baker Eddy b. 1821	S20 10	2 11	14 27	5 05	20 07	
17	W	Billie Holiday d. 1959	R 4 03	2 47	14 59	6 05	20 36	
18	Th	Span. Civil War b'n 1936	S20 07	3 19	15 32	7 06	21 01	
19	F	A.J. Cronin b. 1896	R 4 06	3 53	16 04	8 09	21 25	
20	S	F. Petrarch b. 1304	S20 05	4 26	16 38	9 12	21 48	
21	☙	7th Sunday after Trinity	R 4 08	5 00	17 10	10 17	22 12	
22	M	Bread rationing b'n 1946	S20 02	5 35	17 42	11 23	22 37	
23	Tu	Graham Gooch b. 1953	R 4 11	6 12	18 20	12 30	23 05	
24	W	Freddie Mills d. 1965	S20 00	6 57	19 10	13 39	23 37	
25	Th	James I crowned 1603	R 4 14	7 53	20 17	14 49	—	
26	F	J.B.C. Corot b. 1796	S19 57	9 09	21 41	15 57	0 16	
27	S	Gertrude Stein d. 1946	R 4 17	10 26	22 59	17 02	1 04	
28	☙	8th Sunday after Trinity	S19 54	11 38	—	17 59	2 03	
29	M	Bread rationing end 1948	R 4 19	0 09	12 40	18 49	3 11	
30	Tu	Eng. won World Cup 1966	S19 51	1 08	13 34	19 30	4 28	
31	W	St Ignatius	R 4 22	2 00	14 21	20 06	5 48	

MOON'S PHASES JULY 1996

			Days	Hrs	Mins
○	Full Moon		1	3	58
☾	Last Quarter		7	18	55
●	New Moon		15	16	15
☽	First Quarter		23	17	49
○	Full Moon		30	10	35

All times on this page are GMT (Add 1 hour BST)

PREDICTIONS

The Full Moon on the 1st is in Capricorn, is square to Saturn and falls on the 7th cusp at Westminster, indicating a major Parliamentary row over foreign policy. This will include relations with the European Union. The government will bow to public opinion, and could be considering a referendum on European integration. This is a critical moment internationally and any disputes not settled now could lead to outright hostility by early August. All the major global powers are concerned, chiefly Britain, the USA, France, Germany and Russia.

The New Moon on the 15th falls in Cancer, in opposition to Neptune, indicating confusion with the banking system, perhaps record losses. There are also likely to be sharp fluctuations in the price of oil, which will be beneficial, through tax revenues, to the British Exchequer.

The Full Moon on the 30th falls in Aquarius, dramatically highlighting Chinese affairs, where the chances of widespread demonstrations, remain for the rest of the year. There will be serious disruption in the Middle East, with revolutionary change in both Israel and Syria.

At Goodwood Races the Stewards Cup may be won by a horse carrying 9 st. Favourites should be noted in the non-handicaps.

300th Anniversary Edition on sale July 1996 — Don't miss it!

Predicted the ATOM BOMB on HIROSHIMA, August 1945

AUGUST

For High Water add, for Bristol 5h. 30m., Hull 4h. 23m., Leith 0h. 43m., and for Dublin sub. 2h. 21m., Greenock 1h. 26m., Liverpool 2h. 29m.

D of M	D of W	Sundays, Festivals Special Events, etc., for 1996	Sun Rises R Sets S	High Water at London Bridge Morn.	High Water at London Bridge After.	Moon at London Rises	Moon at London Sets	Weather
			h. m.	h. m.	h. m.	h. m.	h. m.	
1	Th	Parcel post introd. 1883	S19 48	2 48	15 08	20 37	7 10	High temperatures will continue during the first half of the month, but they will give way to spells of heavy rain towards the end.
2	F	Louis Blériot d. 1936	R 4 25	3 36	15 51	21 06	8 29	
3	S	La Scala opened 1778	S19 44	4 21	16 36	21 34	9 47	
4	Su	9th Sunday after Trinity	R 4 29	5 06	17 20	22 02	11 01	
5	M	Bank Holiday, Scotland	S19 41	5 51	18 04	22 32	12 12	
6	Tu	Corinth Canal op. 1893	R 4 32	6 36	18 50	23 06	13 19	
7	W	Mata Hari b. 1876	S19 37	7 26	19 46	23 43	14 21	
8	Th	Great Train Robbery 1963	R 4 35	8 24	20 52	—	15 19	
9	F	Leonide Massine b. 1896	S19 34	9 34	22 17	0 24	16 10	
10	S	Otto Lilienthal d. 1896	R 4 38	10 59	23 35	1 11	16 56	
11	Su	10th Sunday after Trinity	S19 30	—	12 02	2 03	17 35	
12	M	The last quagga d. 1883	R 4 41	0 30	12 50	2 59	18 09	
13	Tu	H.G. Wells d. 1946	S19 26	1 14	13 29	3 58	18 39	
14	W	Bertold Brecht d. 1956	R 4 44	1 50	14 04	4 59	19 06	
15	Th	Princess Royal b. 1950	S19 22	2 24	14 37	6 01	19 31	
16	F	Bela Lugosi d. 1956	R 4 47	2 56	15 09	7 05	19 55	
17	S	George Melly b. 1926	S19 18	3 29	15 40	8 09	20 18	
18	Su	11th Sunday after Trinity	R 4 51	4 01	16 12	9 14	20 42	
19	M	John Flamsteed b. 1646	S19 14	4 34	16 43	10 20	21 09	
20	Tu	Trotsky assassinated 1940	R 4 54	5 07	17 17	11 27	21 39	
21	W	Princess Margaret b. 1930	S19 10	5 42	17 54	12 35	22 15	
22	Th	Honor Blackman b. 1926	R 4 57	6 23	18 40	13 42	22 57	
23	F	Rudolf Valentino d. 1926	S19 05	7 17	19 46	14 46	23 49	
24	S	St Bartholomew	R 5 00	8 33	21 15	15 45	—	
25	Su	12th Sunday after Trinity	S19 01	9 58	22 41	16 37	0 51	
26	M	Bank Holiday, except Scot.	R 5 03	11 17	23 55	17 21	2 01	
27	Tu	Titian d. 1576	S18 57	—	12 23	18 00	3 18	
28	W	John Houston d. 1988	R 5 06	0 56	13 18	18 33	4 39	
29	Th	Michael Jackson b. 1958	S18 53	1 46	14 06	19 04	6 00	
30	F	Raymond Massey b. 1896	R 5 10	2 33	14 49	19 33	7 20	
31	S	Henry Moore d. 1986	S18 48	3 18	15 32	20 02	8 37	

MOON'S PHASES AUGUST 1996

		Days	*Hrs*	*Mins*
☾	Last Quarter	6	5	25
●	New Moon	14	7	34
☽	First Quarter	22	3	36
○	Full Moon	28	17	52

All times on this page are GMT (Add 1 hour BST)

PREDICTIONS

The New Moon on the 14th is in Leo, and falls in the eleventh house at Westminster. Venus and Mars are opposed to Jupiter and squared to Saturn. This is a complex financial indicator, coinciding with very mixed indications from the stock exchange; it is likely that a fall in prices may be precipitated around the 10th. Agricultural subsidies are also likely to be cut. There is prolonged instability in Russia, with outlying republics in dispute with Moscow. The US will be involved in a military adventure, but could also be distracted by problems in California, perhaps race riots. Some shipping losses can be expected.

The Full Moon on the 28th is in Pisces, is square to Pluto, and falls in the first house at Westminster, causing possible problems associated with the Church; there will be the first moves to appoint a female bishop. Serbia will be attempting to create a formal union with the Serb regions of Bosnia and Croatia, although this is unlikely to be finalised until June 1997. There could be a change of government in Germany and serious and disruptive arguments in the European Union. There could be an army mutiny in Egypt.

At York Races the Ebor Handicap may be won by a horse carrying 8 st 2 lbs.

OLD MOORE'S predictions are world famous

27 September, total eclipse of the Moon, 01h.13m – 04h.35m.

Financial Shock

Nuclear Accidents

Under Pressure

SEPTEMBER

For High Water add, for Bristol 5h. 30m., Hull 4h. 23m., Leith 0h. 43m., and for Dublin sub. 2h. 21m., Greenock 1h. 26m., Liverpool 2h. 29m.

D of M	D of W	Sundays, Festivals Special Events, etc., for 1996	Sun Rises R Sets S	High Water at London Bridge Morn.	High Water at London Bridge After.	Moon at London Rises	Moon at London Sets	Weather
			h. m.	h. m.	h. m.	h. m.	h. m.	
1	�	13th Sunday after Trinity	R 5 13	4 00	16 14	20 33	9 52	
2	M	Jimmy Connors b. 1952	S18 44	4 41	16 55	21 05	11 03	
3	Tu	Treaty of Paris 1783	R 5 16	5 21	17 35	21 42	12 09	
4	W	Forth road br. op. 1964	S18 39	6 02	18 18	22 22	13 10	
5	Th	Freddy Mercury b. 1946	R 5 19	6 46	19 08	23 08	14 04	
6	F	Jacky Trent b. 1940	S18 35	7 39	20 11	23 58	14 52	
7	S	Buddy Holly b. 1936	R 5 22	8 45	21 32	—	15 34	
8	☸	14th Sunday after Trinity	S18 30	10 12	23 04	0 53	16 10	
9	M	D. Tutu enthroned 1986	R 5 26	11 31	—	1 50	16 42	
10	Tu	Charles Cruft d. 1938	S18 26	0 04	12 22	2 51	17 10	
11	W	O. Henry b. 1982	R 5 29	0 47	13 03	3 53	17 35	
12	Th	MOT tests introd. 1960	S18 21	1 24	13 38	4 56	17 59	
13	F	B. of Marathon 490 BC	R 5 32	1 56	14 10	6 00	18 23	
14	S	Jewish New Year	S18 16	2 28	14 41	7 05	18 48	
15	☸	15th Sunday after Trinity	R 5 35	3 01	15 13	8 12	19 14	
16	M	James Jeans d. 1946	S18 12	3 33	15 46	9 19	19 43	
17	Tu	Pat Phoenix d. 1986	R 5 38	4 07	16 19	10 26	20 16	
18	W	Frankie Avalon b. 1939	S18 07	4 41	16 55	11 33	20 56	
19	Th	Visc. Leverhulme b. 1851	R 5 42	5 17	17 34	12 37	21 44	
20	F	Jelly Roll Morton b. 1885	S18 02	5 59	18 25	13 36	22 40	
21	S	Autumn equinox 18h 00m	R 5 45	6 53	19 32	14 29	23 45	
22	☸	16th Sunday after Trinity	S17 58	8 09	20 59	15 15	—	
23	M	Day of Atonement	R 5 48	9 36	22 25	15 54	0 56	
24	Tu	Scott Fitzgerald b. 1896	S17 53	10 59	23 40	16 29	2 13	
25	W	Felicity Kendal b. 1946	R 5 51	—	12 05	17 01	3 32	
26	Th	Leonard Sachs b. 1946	S17 49	0 39	13 00	17 30	4 51	
27	F	IMF established 1945	R 5 54	1 29	13 46	17 59	6 10	
28	S	1st day of Tabernacles	S17 44	2 14	14 30	18 29	7 27	
29	☸	17th Sunday after Trinity	R 5 58	2 56	15 11	19 02	8 41	
30	M	Michael Innes b. 1906	S17 40	3 36	15 50	19 37	9 51	

The weather will be dry, calm and sunny up to around the 15th. Then we can expect autumnal gales and a fall in temperature.

PREDICTIONS

The New Moon on the 12th is in Virgo and falls in the fourth house at Westminster, coinciding with measures to stabilise the housing market. There is uncertainty, with falling prices still a problem in parts of the country. There is also likely to be a financial shock. The period around the 9th brings a heightened possibility of earth tremors, random terrorist attacks or nuclear accidents, with Germany and Japan being the most sensitive regions. In Russia there will be moves to reformulate the Commonwealth of Independent States. The Balkans once again come to the centre of the world stage.

The Full Moon on the 27th is a lunar eclipse, is an exact conjunction with Saturn and falls in the eighth house at Westminster, indicating financial troubles, probably a weakening in the trade balance or a shortfall in government revenue. This will dramatically alter the Chancellor's budget calculations, removing chances of tax cuts. In Japan there could be constitutional problems, probably concerning the country's military role, and the pressure to commit Japan's soldiers overseas. There could be a new prime minister in France.

At Doncaster Races the St. Leger may be won by the favourite, and the Doncaster Cup also by the favourite.

MOON'S PHASES SEPTEMBER 1996			Days	Hrs	Mins
☾	Last Quarter		4	19	6
●	New Moon		14	23	07
☽	First Quarter		20	11	23
○	Full Moon		27	2	51

All times on this page are GMT (Add 1 hour BST)

1997 RAPHAEL'S ASTROLOGICAL ALMANAC on sale September 1996

12 October, partial eclipse of the Sun, 12h.00m – 16h.05m.

Business & Law

Germany

Radical Change

OCTOBER

For High Water add, for Bristol 5h. 30m., Hull 4h. 23m..
Leith 0h. 43m., and for Dublin sub. 2h. 21m..
Greenock 1h. 26m., Liverpool 2h. 29m.

D of M	D of W	Sundays, Festivals Special Events, etc., for 1996	Sun Rises R Sets S	High Water at London Bridge Morn.	After.	Moon at London Rises	Sets	Wea-ther
			h. m.	h. m.	h. m.	h. m.	h. m.	
1	Tu	Vladimir Horowitz b. 1904	R 6 01	4 14	16 28	20 17	10 56	
2	W	Mahatma Gandi b. 1869	S17 35	4 52	17 07	21 01	11 54	
3	Th	William Morris d. 1896	R 6 04	5 28	17 48	21 51	12 46	
4	F	J.-F. Millet b. 1814	S17 30	6 08	18 34	22 44	13 31	
5	S	Jarrow March started 1936	R 6 07	6 56	19 34	23 41	14 09	
6	☾	18th Sunday after Trinity	S17 26	7 59	20 47	—	14 42	
7	M	Carbon paper patent 1806	R 6 11	9 18	22 14	0 40	15 12	
8	Tu	St Bridget	S17 22	10 46	23 26	1 41	15 38	
9	W	Steve Ovett b. 1955	R 6 14	11 47	—	2 44	16 03	
10	Th	Charles Dance b. 1946	S17 17	0 12	12 29	3 48	16 27	
11	F	Anton Bruckner d. 1896	R 6 18	0 50	13 05	4 53	16 51	
12	S	St Felix	S17 13	1 25	13 38	6 00	17 17	
13	☾	19th Sunday after Trinity	R 6 21	1 57	14 11	7 08	17 45	
14	M	Lillian Gish b. 1896	S17 08	2 33	14 47	8 17	18 18	
15	Tu	Goering's suicide 1946	R 6 24	3 06	15 22	9 25	18 56	
16	W	Nuremberg hangings 1946	S17 04	3 41	15 58	10 31	19 41	
17	Th	Calder Hall opened 1956	R 6 28	4 19	16 39	11 32	20 35	
18	F	Mart. Navratilova b. 1956	S17 00	4 59	17 24	12 26	21 36	
19	S	King John d. 1216	R 6 31	5 44	18 18	13 13	22 44	
20	☾	20th Sunday after Trinity	S16 56	6 40	19 26	13 54	23 57	
21	M	Aberfan disaster 1966	R 6 35	7 53	20 47	14 29	—	
22	Tu	Paul Cézanne d. 1906	S16 52	9 16	22 08	15 00	1 13	
23	W	Hungarian uprising 1956	R 6 38	10 36	23 20	15 29	2 30	
24	Th	Sir Fred Pontin b. 1906	S16 48	11 44	—	15 58	3 46	
25	F	G. Chaucer b.1340/d.1400	R 6 42	0 20	12 40	16 27	5 03	
26	S	F. Mitterand b. 1916	S16 44	1 11	13 28	16 57	6 17	
27	☾	21st Sunday after Trinity	R 6 45	1 55	14 10	17 31	7 29	
28	M	Escoffier, chef, b. 1846	S16 40	2 35	14 49	18 09	8 38	
29	Tu	Raleigh executed 1618	R 6 49	3 13	15 27	18 52	9 40	
30	W	Diego Maradona b. 1960	S16 36	3 49	16 05	19 40	10 36	
31	Th	Hallowe'en	R 6 52	4 24	16 42	20 33	11 25	

(Weather column, running vertically:) An Indian summer can be expected for the first ten days or so, followed by showery outbreaks around mid-month and a return to a colder spell.

MOON'S PHASES OCTOBER 1996			Days	Hrs	Mins
	☽	Last Quarter	4	12	4
	●	New Moon	12	14	14
	☽	First Quarter	19	18	9
	○	Full Moon	26	14	11

All times GMT (BST to Oct 27 + 1 hr)

PREDICTIONS

The New Moon on the 12th is in Libra and in the eighth house at Westminster, inaugurating a period in which financial matters, concerning banks, mortgages, insurance, taxes and related issues will dominate the headlines. There are likely to be serious discussions prior to the 12th, probably resulting in cuts in interest rates. Instability in Russia continues. As the month opens the US could be involved in a trade war, and there are fears of trade barriers and a new protectionism. This fact may well lead to a new series of talks, hastily convened.

The Full Moon on the 26th is in Taurus and is in an exact square to Uranus bringing the risk of earth tremors and political earthquakes. In Britain, there are complicated problems linking business to the law. Expect a financial scandal, but also serious problems concerning the costs of prison and justice systems. If the government tries to save money, perhaps cutting the cost of legal aid, it is likely to be rejected in the courts. There could be radical changes in Germany, probably a shift in foreign policy.

At Newmarket Races the Cambridgeshire may be won by a horse carrying 8 st 1 lb, and the Cesarewitch by the second favourite.

Clocks back 1 hour, 27 October

Predicted Disintegration of Yugoslavia 1992

ELECTION DAY

NOVEMBER

For High Water add, for Bristol 5h. 30m., Hull 4h. 23m., Leith 0h. 43m., and for Dublin sub. 2h. 21m., Greenock 1h. 26m., Liverpool 2h. 29m.

D of M	D of W	Sundays, Festivals Special Events, etc., for 1996	Sun Rises R Sets S	High Water at London Bridge Morn.	After.	Moon at London Rises	Sets	Weather
			h. m.	h. m.	h. m.	h. m.	h. m.	
1	F	Pony Club founded 1929	S16 33	4 57	17 21	21 29	12 06	.
2	S	J. Carter elected 1976	R 6 56	5 34	18 05	22 27	12 42	
3	☙	22nd Sunday after Trinity	S16 29	6 18	18 57	23 28	13 13	
4	M	UNESCO estab. 1946	R 6 59	7 14	20 02	—	13 40	
5	Tu	Guy Fawkes Night	S16 26	8 26	21 13	0 30	14 05	
6	W	Catharine the Gt d. 1796	R 7 03	9 43	22 25	1 33	14 29	
7	Th	Joan Sutherland b. 1926	S16 22	10 52	23 23	2 37	14 53	
8	F	Beer Hall *Putsch* 1923	R 7 06	11 44	—	3 43	15 18	
9	S	Edward VII b. 1841	S16 19	0 09	12 26	4 51	15 45	
10	☙	Remembrance Sunday	R 7 10	0 49	13 05	6 01	16 16	
11	M	Home Guard disband 1944	S16 16	1 28	13 43	7 11	16 52	
12	Tu	Neil Young b. 1946	R 7 13	2 06	14 23	8 20	17 36	
13	W	St Homobonus	S16 13	2 45	15 02	9 24	18 27	
14	Th	Prince of Wales b. 1948	R 7 17	3 23	15 44	10 23	19 28	
15	F	NBC inaug. (US) 1926	S16 10	4 05	16 29	11 13	20 35	
16	S	Oswald Mosley b. 1896	R 7 20	4 49	17 19	11 56	21 47	
17	☙	24th Sunday after Trinity	S16 08	5 37	18 15	12 33	23 02	
18	M	King's Cross fire 1987	R 7 23	6 33	19 18	13 04	—	
19	Tu	Charles I b. 1600	S16 05	7 39	20 30	13 33	0 17	
20	W	Snowdonia a Nat. Park	R 7 27	8 52	21 44	14 01	1 32	
21	Th	Goldie Hawn b. 1945	S16 03	10 10	22 56	14 28	2 47	
22	F	Jack London d. 1916	R 7 30	11 20	23 58	14 57	4 00	
23	S	Diana Quick b. 1946	S16 01	—	12 19	15 29	5 12	
24	☙	25th Sunday after Trinity	R 7 33	0 50	13 08	16 04	6 21	
25	M	Andrew Carnegie b. 1835	S15 59	1 35	13 52	16 44	7 26	
26	Tu	Tommy Dorsey d. 1956	R 7 36	2 16	14 31	17 30	8 25	
27	W	John Major PM 1990	S15 57	2 52	15 09	18 21	9 18	
28	Th	Lucy Gutteridge b. 1946	R 7 39	3 26	15 46	19 16	10 03	
29	F	Derek Jameson b. 1929	S15 56	4 00	16 21	20 14	10 41	
30	S	St Andrew's Day	R 7 42	4 34	16 59	21 14	11 14	

(Weather column, reading vertically): Unfortunately, very mild Novembers such as in 1994 are few and far between. The month will start with a few sunny days, but colder conditions will set in.

MOON'S PHASES NOVEMBER 1996

		Days	Hrs	Mins
☾	Last Quarter	3	7	50
●	New Moon	11	4	16
☽	First Quarter	18	1	9
○	Full Moon	25	4	10

All times on this page are GMT

PREDICTIONS

The New Moon on the 11th falls in Scorpio and is in the second house at Westminster, pointing towards important financial statements. The budget is unlikely to include significant tax cuts, but there may be a botched attempt to settle outstanding housing problems, specifically problems of 'negative equity' and of the cost of paying benefits to home owners. In Russia living standards may be rising, suggesting that economic reforms are working. In the United States the 5th is election day, and the odds are stacked against Clinton being re-elected.

The Full Moon on the 25th is in an exact opposition to Pluto. This raises serious questions concerning international crime. There may be thefts of plutonium or a wider nuclear threat. The harmonious trine between Mars and Jupiter is positive, indicating a beneficial outcome of most disputes. However, there is no end to the strife in Russia, with a breakdown in civil order. In Britain there could be a banking scandal, or even the collapse of a financial institution. Internationally there will be problems with the airline industry, with the chance of a major airline collapse. At Doncaster Races the November Handicap may be won by the second favourite.

Mail a copy of FOULSHAM'S ALMANACK to your friends abroad

Predicted Brighton Bomb attack, 1984

AUTHORITARIAN GOVERNMENTS ENCOURAGED

POPULAR DISCONTENT

DECEMBER

For High Water add, for Bristol 5h. 30m., Hull 4h. 23m.,
Leith 0h. 43m., and for Dublin sub. 2h. 21m.,
Greenock 1h. 26m., Liverpool 2h. 29m.

D of M	D of W	Sundays, Festivals Special Events, etc., for 1996	Sun Rises R Sets S	High Water at London Bridge Morn.	After.	Moon at London Rises	Sets	Weather
			h. m.	h. m.	h. m.	h. m.	h. m.	
1	☉	1st Sunday in Advent	S15 54	5 09	17 38	22 15	11 43	
2	M	Philip Larkin d. 1985	R 7 45	5 47	18 23	23 17	12 08	
3	Tu	Paul Nicholas b. 1946	S15 53	6 32	19 14	—	12 32	
4	W	Samuel Butler b. 1835	R 7 48	7 26	20 16	0 20	12 56	
5	Th	José Carreras b. 1946	S15 52	8 37	21 22	1 25	13 19	
6	F	Ira Gershwin b. 1896	R 7 50	9 47	22 25	2 31	13 45	
7	S	Pearl Harbour 1941	S15 52	10 49	23 21	3 39	14 13	
8	☉	2nd Sunday in Advent	R 7 53	11 42	—	4 49	14 46	
9	M	Kirk Douglas b. 1916	S15 51	0 12	12 33	5 59	15 26	
10	Tu	Alfred Nobel d. 1896	R 7 55	1 00	13 19	7 08	16 15	
11	W	Edward VIII abdic. 1936	S15 51	1 45	14 04	8 11	17 13	
12	Th	Kenya independent 1963	R 7 57	2 28	14 49	9 07	18 19	
13	F	Aga Khan (IV) b. 1936	S15 51	3 11	15 36	9 55	19 33	
14	S	Tycho Brahe b. 1546	R 7 59	3 56	16 22	10 35	20 49	
15	☉	3rd Sunday in Advent	S15 51	4 41	17 13	11 09	22 06	
16	M	Boston Tea Party 1773	R 8 00	5 30	18 05	11 39	23 22	
17	Tu	Tommy Steele b. 1936	S15 52	6 20	19 03	12 07	—	
18	W	Betty Grable b. 1916	R 8 02	7 18	20 06	12 34	0 36	
19	Th	Leonid Brezhnev b. 1906	S15 52	8 24	21 15	13 02	1 49	
20	F	Uri Geller b. 1946	R 8 03	9 37	22 26	13 31	3 00	
21	S	Winter solstice 14h 06m	S15 53	10 52	23 33	14 04	4 09	
22	☉	4th Sunday in Advent	R 8 04	11 56	—	14 41	5 15	
23	M	Helmut Schmidt b. 1918	S15 54	0 29	12 50	15 24	6 16	
24	Tu	Christmas Eve	R 8 05	1 17	13 36	16 12	7 11	
25	W	Christmas Day	S15 56	1 57	14 16	17 03	7 59	
26	Th	Boxing Day	R 8 05	2 34	14 52	18 02	8 40	
27	F	Johann Kepler b. 1571	S15 57	3 08	15 27	19 02	9 15	
28	S	Iowa 29th US state 1846	R 8 06	3 40	16 03	20 03	9 46	
29	☉	1st Sunday after Christmas	S15 59	4 12	16 38	21 04	10 13	
30	M	Rasputin d. 1916	R 8 06	4 46	17 13	22 07	10 37	
31	Tu	New Year's Eve	S16 01	5 21	17 51	23 10	11 00	

(Weather column, running vertically): 'Chill December brings the sleet, blazing hearths, Christmas treat' sums up this month aptly. But a few reasonably mild days can be expected.

MOON'S PHASES DECEMBER 1996

			Days	Hrs	Mins
☾	Last Quarter		3	5	6
●	New Moon		10	16	56
☽	First Quarter		17	9	31
○	Full Moon		24	20	41

All times on this page are GMT

PREDICTIONS

The New Moon on the 10th is in Sagittarius and is in square to Mars and semi-sextile Jupiter, encouraging arguments of principle and religious disputes, though even when hostilities break out they could be settled very quickly. The regions under greatest pressure include Chile, southeast Asia and south-central Africa, including Angola, where there will be another peace agreement between the warring parties. In Britain, the extension of employment rights are likely to be extended, with large additional costs for business. Unpopular measures taken by the government will attract significant interest from disaffected members of the ruling party.

The Full Moon on the 24th falls in a square to Saturn, encouraging authoritarian governments, although it looks as if firstly people at large will be happy to accept authority, and secondly that, if challenged, authority may prove weaker than it appears. In Russia nationalist pressure is again at a peak and it seems unlikely whether the concept of Russia as an independent, democratic state, can survive. The government's authority may be seriously limited in the face of popular discontent.

The King George VI Chase at Kempton may be won by the favourite.

OLD MOORE for all the family

. . 47 . .

Cont'd from p.33

LEO BORN PEOPLE

AUGUST   The best month for Leo successes, not least of all because the Sun is back in your part of the sky. Adventures are likely and you probably feel more dynamic than has been the case for quite some time. Fortune favours quick, frequent efforts on your part and does not respond to much deep thinking for the moment. At the same time your constitution needs a little rest from time to time.
Love 18, 19. Fortune 24, 25. Health 2, 3. Recharge 9, 10.

SEPTEMBER   You settle to routines much easier now, and may not be quite so inclined to seek out fresh fields and pastures new. Arguments can crop up, and particularly so if you are not doing what other people demand of you. Trends show a more stubborn Lion, which doesn't really help at all. Look for patience, tact and diplomacy. It may be a fruitless search but is worth the effort.
Love 16, 17. Fortune 22, 23. Health 29, 30. Recharge 7, 8.

OCTOBER   You never do suffer fools gladly, and especially not at the start of October. The attitude of others has a great bearing on the way that you are feeling yourself and the colour of the world outside your door is reflected in your own life. Perhaps you are too much influenced by others and could do with choosing for yourself more now. Towards the end of the month you should come across some better luck.
Love 14, 15. Fortune 20, 21. Health 27, 28. Recharge 5, 6.

NOVEMBER   Now that you rank so highly in the estimation of others, you are in a position to make more of yourself and your life generally. Work steadily towards your objectives, and look out for Capricorn people, with whom you have much in common at present. Treat November as a month to make endings and beginnings. Time spent on your own is certainly not wasted, even if it might appear to be.
Love 12, 13. Fortune 18, 19. Health 25, 26. Recharge 3, 4.

DECEMBER   It's only when you actually arrive at the end of the year that you realise the sort of progress that you have made. A much more dynamic Lion is now around and is on view to the whole world. Leave arrangements for Christmas to others, whilst you work on steadily, right up until the last moment. If you can't have everything the way you want it to be, you can give a good impression!
Love 10, 11. Fortune 16, 17. Health 23, 24. Recharge 1, 2.

VIRGO BORN PEOPLE

Birthdays between August 24th and September 23rd inclusive. Your planet is Mercury. Birthstone, sardonyx. Lucky day, Wednesday.

SUN–MOON CYCLES: All astrology depends on cycles, and at the end of each month in the readings below, you will find a series of diary dates, each connected with the commencement of a two-day cycle that relates to the moving Moon and its association with your Sun sign. The dates listed are headed **Love, Fortune, Health** and **Recharge**. The first three indicate times when effort really pays out in the area concerned, whilst **Recharge** means putting in less effort and taking a break from pressure.

JANUARY   Yours can be a deep and complex sign, and sometimes too much inclined to worry over details. Try to start the year on a lighthearted note and you cannot go far wrong. The Virgo attention to detail is certainly in evidence, and this means successes through concentration, hard work and a total belief in your own abilities. Leave time for romance towards the end of the month.
Love 28, 29. Fortune 6, 7. Health 14, 15. Recharge 21, 22.

FEBRUARY   Astrologers spend a good deal of time telling people that it is trends, rather than specific happenings, that are the most important facts in a person's life. How true this is for Virgo this month. You can either use your energies, which are great, for the benefit of everyone you come across, or keep them for your own selfish ends. The power is the same, but how you use it is up to you.
Love 28, 29. Fortune 6, 7. Health 14, 15. Recharge 21, 22.

VIRGO BORN PEOPLE

MARCH A very much less intense phase is now upon you, so that the chatty, easy going Virgoan puts in a lengthy appearance at about this time. Routines mean very much less to you and you are likely to act on impulse much more than you normally would. This makes you good to be with, cheerful and quite delightful to know. You do need to plan well ahead though, especially concerning travel.
Love 28, 29. Fortune 6, 7. Health 14, 15. Recharge 21, 22.

APRIL Give and take appear to be the hallmarks of your sign during the spring, so that you can forgive others almost anything and gain yourself more popularity on the way. Money matters see you being quite careful, but also gaining from limited speculations. An atmospheric period, when your intuition is strong and when you find that what you know instinctively counts more than acquired knowledge.
Love 26, 27. Fortune 4, 5. Health 12, 13. Recharge 19, 20.

MAY Try to relax as much as possible. There are trends around that could indicate the return of a more worrisome Virgoan, which would be a pity after such a long period when you refused to allow minor issues to get you down. Acting on impulse is always good for you, and there is a period around the 20th when this is especially useful. Perhaps the best month of all for planning journeys.
Love 25, 26. Fortune 2, 3. Health 10, 11. Recharge 17, 18.

JUNE All sorts of minor irritations and restrictions threaten to get in your way at present, though of course, you do not have to respond to them if you do not wish to do so. Words of encouragement are always at hand, whilst the possibilities of love are especially rewarding. Wild and lonely natural settings have a particular appeal to you at this time, with or without friends.
Love 23, 24. Fortune 29, 30. Health 8, 9. Recharge 15, 16.

JULY Forgive yourself immediately if you do not always come up to your own high standards during July. The problem, if there is one, is that you are feeling wild and free, and quite unable to take life in the serious way that is most comfortable for you. Life is a merry-go-round and the best thing that you can do during July is to enjoy the ride as much as possible. Who needs endless responsibilities anyway?
Love 21, 22. Fortune 27, 28. Health 6, 7. Recharge 13, 14.

AUGUST If advancement is what you are after, you could just find yourself in the right place and time to find it. You are bound to be concentrating more now on the job in hand and will find plenty to keep you occupied throughout the whole of August. Make time for travel howeever, since the trends in this direction are extremely strong and fortunate. Minor health problems, if they occur, will soon pass.
Love 19, 20. Fortune 25, 26. Health 4, 5. Recharge 11, 12.

SEPTEMBER Suddenly others are very important to you, so that if there is a month this year when you really need to be part of the group, this is it. Constant appeals to your better nature from people who could do more for themselves do raise a typical Virgoan resentment, though you can find ways to curb this. Steady and secure most of the time, financial gains probably come as a result of careful planning.
Love 17, 18. Fortune 23, 24. Health 2, 3. Recharge 9, 10.

OCTOBER A fixed and rigid attitude towards anything is certainly not to be recommended for October, even if it takes everything you have to avoid this sort of thinking. There are many different paths towards the same destination, and your effort now should be given to looking at those devised by other people. Better financial luck is on the way, and fortune smiles on your efforts to make changes at home.
Love 15, 16. Fortune 21, 22. Health 29, 30. Recharge 7, 8.

NOVEMBER November will probably be quiet, but nevertheless eventful in a low-key sort of way. You can train yourself to see below the surface of the pond of life and to find an entirely different world as a result. If famous people cross your path, you should be able to make use of their appearance in your own universe. Dismissing your own good ideas out of hand would not be sensible right now.
Love 13, 14. Fortune 19, 20. Health 27, 28. Recharge 5, 6.

VIRGO BORN PEOPLE

DECEMBER You now keep one destination at once in your mind, and it's unlikely that anyone could persuade you to abandon something that you really believe in, even if you know that you could be wrong. We all have to make our own mistakes, but by the middle of the month you are far more flexible and probably really looking forward to what the Christmas period has to offer. The warm and loving responses of those in your vicinity can be a distinct help.
Love 11, 12. Fortune 17, 18. Health 25, 26. Recharge 3, 4.

LIBRA BORN PEOPLE

Birthdays between September 24th and October 23rd inclusive. Your planet is Venus. Birthstone, opal. Lucky day, Friday.

SUN–MOON CYCLES: All astrology depends on cycles, and at the end of each month in the readings below, you will find a series of diary dates, each connected with the commencement of a two-day cycle that relates to the moving Moon and its association with your Sun sign. The dates listed are headed **Love, Fortune, Health** and **Recharge**. The first three indicate times when effort really pays out in the area concerned, whilst **Recharge** means putting in less effort and taking a break from pressure.

JANUARY A good way for Libra to start the year, with most astrological cycles working distinctly to your advantage. Shelve a tendency to look back too much, because you find yourself in a phase when projecting yourself forward is all important. Reversals only confirm that you are walking on the right path and that you have a year of happiness and surprises now ahead of you.
Love 5, 6. Fortune 12, 13. Health 19, 20. Recharge 25, 26.

FEBRUARY Although the start of February could seem slightly less inspiring, the more so because you are not a lover of darkest winter, in the main you show a positive face to the world. Your greatest gift is diplomacy, something that really comes into its own during this month. Not only are you capable of feathering your own nest, but you have the power to help others on the way.
Love 3, 4. Fortune 10, 11. Health 17, 18. Recharge 23, 24.

MARCH March should be inspiring and probably less gloomy than earlier weeks tended to be. You are always good to have around, and since the message of 1996 is to take what you have and to use it to the full, make the most of your sunny nature when with others. You have a great need to be noticed at this time, a fact that is not lost on the world. Probably a secure month financially.
Love 3, 4. Fortune 10, 11. Health 17, 18. Recharge 23, 24.

APRIL When it really counts the most you have the ability to pull out all the stops and to show what you are really capable of. This quality is especially important in April. There are times when it seems as though life is not working with you, yet it is possible to not only turn difficulties round, but to succeed despite them. The power to do so lies deep inside you now.
Love 1, 2. Fortune 8, 9. Health 15, 16. Recharge 21, 22.

MAY Trends are variable at this time and it is sometimes difficult for you to know how to react. The answer lies within your own intuition, which is strengthened around May time and which should turn out to be your best guide. Not everyone is going to be equally helpful and you may have to make allowances for the fact. Romance should shine strongly in your life towards the end of the month.
Love 30, 31. Fortune 6, 7. Health 13, 14. Recharge 19, 20.

JUNE There is little wonder that you are so well loved by others. As bright and cheerful as June itself, there is very little that now lies beyond your capabilities, as long as you have faith. If you can conceive an idea, chances are that you can follow it through. When problems do arise at present you are inclined to either laugh at them, or to deal with them in an imaginative way.
Love 28, 29. Fortune 4, 5. Health 11, 12. Recharge 17, 18.

LIBRA BORN PEOPLE

JULY Although July might be quieter, there is scope for advancement at work, for travel and also for personal rewards. You may find it difficult to make quite the impression on the world at large that you did earlier in the year, but this short interlude does at least offer the possibility of rest, something you never get enough of. Long distance travel would prove to be especially good.
Love 26, 27. Fortune 2, 3. Health 9, 10. Recharge 15, 16.

AUGUST Stand quietly on the outside of almost any situation that looks as though it could prove difficult and take your time before launching yourself into action. The adage, 'It seemed like a good idea at the time' is present now, and can lead to some upsets. Routines might get in the way of having a good time, but not if you deal with them in your customary cheerful, zippy way.
Love 24, 25. Fortune 30, 31. Health 7, 8. Recharge 13, 14.

SEPTEMBER Words of love are important in September, not only the ones you whisper to others, but also those that are coming back at you. Anything that makes you have more confidence in yourself right now can only turn out to be a good thing. Look out for creative urges, which set this month apart and allow you to look at your home surroundings, and probably other areas of life too, in a new way.
Love 22, 23. Fortune 28, 29. Health 5, 6. Recharge 11, 12.

OCTOBER October might not be the most inspiring month of the year, but it does have particular advantages of its own, not least of all in terms of the slow and steady progress which is important to everyone. True, you probably won't be moving any mountains, because trends don't favour drastic actions. What you can do is to get plenty of rest and to take an interest in the world around you.
Love 20, 21. Fortune 26, 27. Health 3, 4. Recharge 9, 10.

NOVEMBER The year is getting older, whilst most Libran subjects appear to be getting younger every day. Your zest for life has probably not been greater, so most of the month finds you in full swing and anxious to have a go at almost anything. Now more sensible than ever, you do have bouts of silliness as well, though even these can be turned to your advantage if you think about them.
Love 18, 94. Fortune 24, 25. Health 1, 2. Recharge 7, 8.

DECEMBER If other people believe in you, then your own confidence, such an important component to 1996, grows as a result. Listen to what is being said about you, because compliments should not be in short supply at this stage. Creating the right sort of atmosphere for the Christmas period is important, though you are probably so busy in other ways you will be happy to leave the details to others.
Love 16, 17. Fortune 22, 23. Health 30, 31. Recharge 5, 6.

SCORPIO BORN PEOPLE

Birthdays between October 24th and November 22nd inclusive. Your planets are Mars and Pluto. Birthstone, topaz. Lucky day, Tuesday.

SUN–MOON CYCLES: All astrology depends on cycles, and at the end of each month in the readings below, you will find a series of diary dates, each connected with the commencement of a two-day cycle that relates to the moving Moon and its association with your Sun sign. The dates listed are headed **Love, Fortune, Health** and **Recharge**. The first three indicate times when effort really pays out in the area concerned, whilst **Recharge** means putting in less effort and taking a break from pressure.

JANUARY If events seem to hold you back at the start of the year, you will need a bigger push than ever to get through or round them. Attitude is all important to the cycles that surround you now and your successes are due, in great measure, to your own effort. Later in the month you should find finances improving, and that could mean more freedom to please yourself. Stay optimistic.
Love 8, 9. Fortune 15, 16. Health 21, 22. Recharge 27, 28.

.. 54 ..

SCORPIO BORN PEOPLE

FEBRUARY A few refreshing changes to routines could make February seem more exciting than it starts out being. The patterns of life are weaving intricate designs around you all the time, allowing a greater sense of personal freedom and also posing some challenges that you are happy to rise to. Love and relationships take up some of your time, as yuou try to sort out the actions of others.
Love 6, 7. Fortune 13, 14. Health 19, 20. Recharge 25, 26.

MARCH Creating space as the spring arrives, you should find that you are able to put the finishing touches to plans that have been on your mind for quite a while. Agreements with others come easy, for there is no sign of an argumentative Scorpio at the moment. You are easy to love now, and tend to be displaying a good deal of affection in return. Don't be held back by negative types.
Love 6, 7. Fortune 13, 14. Health 19, 20. Recharge 25, 26.

APRIL All things being equal, April may prove to be the most positive month of the year in a financial sense. Even if money does not actually come your way now, you do have the ability to sow the seeds of schemes that bring cash to you later. Few could doubt your enthusiasm, or your ability to see things through to the end. Really important ventures should certainly not be left until later.
Love 4, 5. Fortune 11, 12. Health 17, 18. Recharge 23, 24.

MAY As May opens the door on the summer, so you could find yourself growing slightly more restless and anxious to ring the changes in some way. Such restless spells are inevitable on occasions and should not be taken too seriously. Keeping up a break-neck pace, you could tire easily later in the month, and if so, more rest is prescribed. Fortune smiles on your ability to back your hunches.
Love 2, 3. Fortune 9, 10. Health 15, 16. Recharge 21, 22.

JUNE June finds you in a fairly good frame of mind, even if the same cannot always be said for the people living and working around you. The only slight problem is that you may spend so many hours convincing others to remain cheerful, that there is little time left to think about yourself. A more confident approach generally gradually begins to take you over as the weeks pass.
Love 29, 30. Fortune 7, 8. Health 13, 14. Recharge 19, 20.

JULY Keep to tried and tested paths, if only for the start of July. There is nothing to prevent you from putting a toe into the water of life, but you may not feel like taking too many chances all at once. Contributing to a more confident approach by those around you, there are gains to be made as a result of their actions. When you do take a back seat, you are still making progress.
Love 27, 28. Fortune 5, 6. Health 11, 12. Recharge 17, 18.

AUGUST August brings the best trends for travel and for making necessary changes around your home. There might not be all that much time to think, so it's fair to say that actions count for the most. Stronger financial trends should soon be in the offing and you have plenty of energy to take on new projects. Not a good time for allowing yourself to get stuck in any sort of rut.
Love 25, 26. Fortune 3, 4. Health 9, 10. Recharge 15, 16.

SEPTEMBER More progressive than ever, there is very little time for the introspective sort of Scorpio to put in an appearance at this time. Advantages come thick and fast, and from a number of different directions. Taking anything slowly and steadily now may prove to be almost impossible, and you only have to control the forces that are at work around you in order to gain from them.
Love 23, 24. Fortune 1, 2. Health 7, 8. Recharge 13, 14.

OCTOBER The season of mists and mellow fruitfulness could not be more aptly named in your case. October promises to be the repository of many of your hopes for the year up to now. Don't be afraid to take the rewards that are owing to you, particularly since others are so willing to offer them. It's good to give, but receiving can be necesssary too. This is your single most important lesson now.
Love 21, 22. Fortune 30, 31. Health 5, 6. Recharge 11, 12.

SCORPIO BORN PEOPLE

NOVEMBER A slightly less eventful month could be on offer, though this does not mean that you should fail to respond to the very many positive trends that are around you at present. You need to be quite sure about your actions before you commit yourself to any long-term changes, and this may not be the month for them. A casual, and even off-hand approach might tend to suit you best.
Love 19, 20. Fortune 28, 29. Health 3, 4. Recharge 9, 10.

DECEMBER Although you cannot be certain how other people will react to your ideas at the start of December, trends being what they are it should not take long for you to find out. Be definite in your ideas about the festive season and plan early in the month for any grandiose schemes. Confidence should not be hard to find and you might also discover that finances are strengthening.
Love 17, 18. Fortune 26, 27. Health 1, 2. Recharge 7, 8.

SAGITTARIUS BORN PEOPLE

Birthdays between November 23rd and December 21st inclusive.
Your planet is Jupiter. Birthstone, turquoise. Lucky day, Thursday.

SUN–MOON CYCLES: All astrology depends on cycles, and at the end of each month in the readings below, you will find a series of diary dates, each connected with the commencement of a two-day cycle that relates to the moving Moon and its association with your Sun sign. The dates listed are headed **Love, Fortune, Health** and **Recharge**. The first three indicate times when effort really pays out in the area concerned, whilst **Recharge** means putting in less effort and taking a break from pressure.

JANUARY Yours is a happy and carefree sign when at tis best, which is probably what you can expect at the start of this year. Entertainment and social possibilities are inclined to take up a fair percentage of your time, though trends towards a greater control of your professional life are in evidence later. Perhaps not everyone altogether understands you at the present time.
Love 10, 11. Fortune 17, 18. Health 24, 25. Recharge 29, 30.

FEBRUARY You should feel that you are coming to terms with those around you rather better now, though if you are, this probably has more to do with your own attitude than with theirs. With a greater tendency to wear your optimism like a badge, there is a chance that the best qualities of the Archer are now on display. You should have more control over your own financial prospects.
Love 8, 9. Fortune 15, 16. Health 22, 23. Recharge 27, 28.

MARCH The prospect of the spring should warm you through no end, and, together with the aspects that attend its arrival, may also cause you to make significant changes to your life in a practical sense. The bravery that your sign is so capable of displaying is definitely in evidence right now, and you are unlikely to back away from a potential argument at any stage during March.
Love 8, 9. Fortune 15, 16. Health 22, 23. Recharge 27, 28.

APRIL Planetary positions in your solar chart should cause you to take more notice of what is going on around you in the world at this stage, so you need to take a broader view of almost every aspect of life right now. Confidence tends to stay quite high and there may be offers of a romantic nature that are both surprising and stimulating. What you do about them is really up to you.
Love 6, 7. Fortune 13, 14. Health 20, 21. Recharge 25, 26.

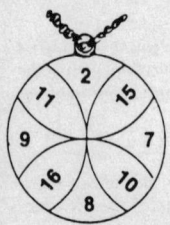
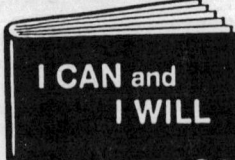

SAGITTARIUS BORN PEOPLE

MAY   Once again, the means to alter situations generally is yours for the taking. However, you tend to be keeping yourself rather busy for the moment, which could easily mean that you have little or no time to be planning carefully. You also tend to be rather outspoken at present, and this might cause others to fight shy of contradicting you. A little more patience might be in order.
Love 4, 5. Fortune 11, 12. Health 18, 19. Recharge 23, 24.

JUNE   Life is a process of learning and growing, no matter if you are six or sixty. Never has this fact been more obvious to you than it is through the early summer months, when practically everything you come across carries a message that you can learn from. This might mean standing and staring on occasions, something which is very good for you, but which you are notoriously bad at doing.
Love 2, 3. Fortune 9, 10. Health 16, 17. Recharge 21, 22.

JULY   A long cycle of minor problems now comes to an end, and although it won't have plagued all Sagittarians, it is worth mentioning because of its disappearance now. This allows you to feel as light as a feather, and to realise that all the hard work has really paid dividends. A good month for travel and for finding fresh fields and pastures new in a mental and spiritual sense too.
Love 29, 30. Fortune 7, 8. Health 14, 15. Recharge 19, 20.

AUGUST   Don't underestimate your own abilities, because you are clearly capable of great things when you put your mind to it. If there is a problem at all during August, it could be that you fail to recognise the fact. Later in the month you are probably more sure of yourself and have great potency in almost any situation. Loved ones and your home should be of special significance now.
Love 27, 28. Fortune 5, 6. Health 12, 13. Recharge 17, 18.

SEPTEMBER   What a busy Sagittarian you are now likely to be. At the same time you could be particularly emotional and not a little nostalgic. All good qualities in their own way, but not if you push yourself so hard that you end up feeling like a wrung out dish cloth. No matter how much you may argue the point now, you are as human as the rest of us, and need to take timeout to rest.
Love 25, 26. Fortune 3, 4. Health 10, 11. Recharge 15, 16.

OCTOBER   You are busy and energetic, at least as the month opens. The autumn should provide some positive opportunities for advancement, but you will need to keep your eye on the ball if you are not to find yourself expecting too much of the world. You forge your own destiny more than most, and especially so now. All the same, there is help on hand if you choose to look for it.
Love 23, 24. Fortune 1, 2. Health 8, 9. Recharge 13, 14.

NOVEMBER   You cannot know what other people are thinking unless you take the trouble to ask them, which is what you should be doing right now. The best ventures now are the cooperative ones at which you excel. Contradictions come in thick and fast, and from a number of different directions. Despite this, November can be both interesting and fortunate, with better than expected results.
Love 21, 22. Fortune 29, 30. Health 6, 7. Recharge 11, 12.

DECEMBER   The ups and downs that have been typical of this year settle down, probably making December one of the quietest months you have encountered. This is not to suggest that life will be dull because there should be plenty to captivate your imagination. Thoughts of Christmas will often keep you fully occupied, though you do need to lay down careful plans for the year that lies ahead.
Love 19, 20. Fortune 27, 28. Health 4, 5. Recharge 9, 10.

HRH THE PRINCESS OF WALES

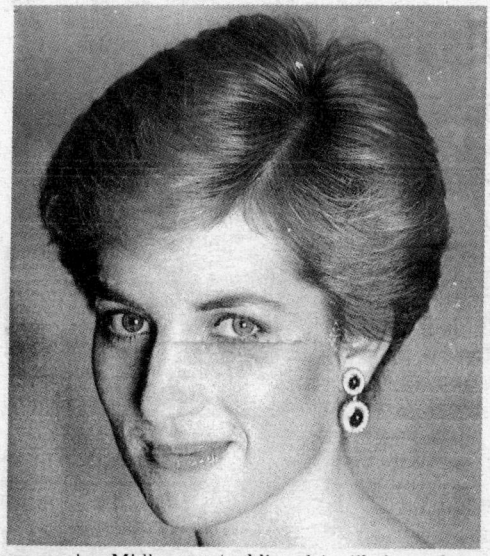

'The queen without a crown' is a fitting title for the 'new' Princess Diana, whose return to public life must make her realise that her role on the world stage is a very powerful one. Surviving the scrutiny of the public and the press is never easy, but after her failed marriage and chilling rejection by the royal family, the princess may now be turning that relentless attention to her own favour. What are the prospects for her new life ahead?

Resilience is one of the outstanding qualities which her Sagittarian Ascendant bestows. Luckily, Jupiter's transit through Sag over her fiery Ascendant and first house throughout '95 and all of '96 is a powerful antidote to the pain and confusion of the past few years. She will have a real ego boost and surge of confidence as she experiences more freedom of choice and movement. Personal constraints undoubtedly still attach to her position—her natal Saturn (duties, limitations) in Capricorn square her Midheaven (public role) will always bring the formal, worldly obligations that go with social status. But Princess Diana is now beginning to feel and use a hard-won maturity, and is realising that the freedom to re-write the rules, even just a *little*, is worth the fight. Jupiter is her ruling planet, and its placement in independent, gregarious Aquarius means that she needs a great deal of direct experience with a wide variety of people. And in the next couple of years, that's just what she is going to get. The public can expect to see Diana globe-trotting in a big way, hob-nobbing with the glamorous, the eccentric, and the down-and-out, and enjoying her flair for *connecting with people* in a new way.

However, her natal Moon-Uranus opposition did not 'fit' into the royal mould, and she was destined to be the black sheep who, in the end, ironically for the royals, scooped all the popularity as well as the liberation. But Diana is not one to shirk her own inner sense of duty, and she is now free to make a *new* relationship with her charity work (she is patron or president of over 100 charities), and will be more committed than ever. The cosmic agenda points to increasing confidence and freedom of choice.

Throughout '96 Diana's progressed Moon is in Gemini, indicating a two-year period of increased travel, communication, and generally being on-the-go. But late '95 and early '96 sees transiting Pluto opposing that Moon and forming a square to her Mars, an aspect of extreme ambition and the instinct to fight. This could be a highly volatile time; she will need to steer a careful course during this period, especially with regards to vitriolic attacks and manoeuvres from those who might be critical or envious of her power. It is quite possible that deteriorating relations with Prince Charles will cause intense frustration, and a widening of the gap in communication could be the result. But in May of '96 Uranus is one-half degree from her Jupiter in wilful, eccentric Aquarius, indicating sudden changes in fortune as well as stimulating opportunities that can make her want to make sweeping changes in her life. The agenda will be laying firm foundations for a future that contains more of *her* desires, *her* happiness, *her* purposes, in short, more of *herself*.

1996 MAIN UNITED KINGDOM FAIRS AND EVENTS

AGRICULTURAL EVENTS

ABERGAVENNY & Border Counties Show — 'Glebelands', Llanwenarth, Abergavenny: 27th July

AYR Show — Ayr Racecourse: 1st-2nd May

BAKEWELL Show: 7th-8th August

BINGLEY Show — Myrtle Park: 7th August

BLACK ISLE Show — Mannsfield Muir-of-Ord, Ross-shire: 1st August

BORDER UNION Show — Springwood Park, Kelso: 26th-27th July

BUCKS County Show — Weedon Park, nr Aylesbury: 5th September

CHESHIRE County Show — Tabley, nr Knutsford: 18th-19th June

DENBIGHSHIRE & FLINTSHIRE Agricultural Society Show — Denbigh: 15th August

DEVON County Show — Westpoint, Clyst St Mary, Exeter: 16th-18th May

DORCHESTER Agricultural Show — Came Park: 7th September

DUMFRIES & LOCKERBIE Show — Park Farm, Dumfries: 3rd August

DURHAM County Agricultural Show — Lambton Park, Chester-le-Street: 13th-14th July

EAST OF ENGLAND Show — Peterborough: 16th-18th July

EGHAM & THORPE Royal Show — Runnymede: 24th-25th August

ESSEX County Show: Great Leighs, nr Chelmsford: 14th-16th June

GREAT YORKSHIRE Show — Harrogate: 11th July

HERTS County Show — Redbourn: 25th-26th May

KENT County Show — Detling, nr Maidstone: 11th-13th July

LEICESTERSHIRE County Show — Dishley Grange Farm, Loughborough: 1st May

LINCOLNSHIRE Show — Grange-de-Lings, Lincoln: 20th June

MONMOUTHSHIRE Show — Monmouth: 24th August

NATIONAL PRIMESTOCK Show & Sale — Bingley Hall, Stafford: 17th-18th November

NATIONAL SHIRE HORSE Show — Peterborough: 16th-17th August

NEW FOREST & HAMPSHIRE Show — Brockenhurst: 30th July-1st August

NEWBURY & ROYAL COUNTY OF BERKSHIRE Show — Chievely, Newbury: 21st-22nd September

NORTH SOMERSET Show — Ashton Court, Bristol: 6th May

NOTTINGHAMSHIRE County Show — Winthorpe, Newark: 3rd-4th May

PEMBROKESHIRE County Show — Withybush, Haverfordwest: 13th-15th August

ROMSEY SHOW — Broadlands Park: 14th September

ROYAL BATH & WEST Show — Shepton Mallet: 29th May-1st June

ROYAL CORNWALL Show — Wadebridge: 6th-8th June

ROYAL HIGHLAND Show — Ingliston, Edinburgh: 20th-23rd June

ROYAL LANCASHIRE Show — Astley Park, Chorley: 26th-28th July (provisional)

ROYAL NORFOLK Show — New Costessey, Norwich: 26th-27th June

ROYAL SHOW — National Agricultural Centre, Stoneleigh Park, Kenilworth: 1st-4th July

ROYAL SMITHFIELD Show — Earls Court: 24th-27th November

ROYAL ULSTER Agricultural Society Balmoral Show — Belfast: 15th-17th May

ROYAL WELSH Show — Llanelwedd, Builth Wells: 22nd-25th July

ST HELENS Show — Sherdley Park: 26th-28th July

ROYAL WELSH AGRICULTURAL WINTER Fair — Llanelwedd, Builth Wells: 3rd December

SHROPSHIRE & WEST MIDLANDS Show — Shrewsbury: 17th-18th May

SOUTH OF ENGLAND Show — Ardingley, Haywards Heath: 6th-8th June

STAFFORDSHIRE County Show — Stafford: 22nd-23rd May

SUFFOLK Show — Ipswich: 29th-30th May

SURREY County Show — Stoke Park, Guildford: 27th May

TENDRING HUNDRED Show — Lawford House Park, nr Manningtree: 13th July

THAME Show: 19th September

THREE COUNTIES Show — Malvern: 11th-13th June

TOTNES & District Show — Berry Farm, Totnes: 25th July

TURRIFF Show — The Haughs: 5th-6th August

UNITED COUNTIES Show — Nantyci Showground, Carmarthen: 9th-10th August

WESTMORLAND County Show — Lane Farm, Crooklands: 12th September

WOKINGHAM & READING Show — Spencer's Wood, nr Reading: 13th September

MISCELLANEOUS

ALDEBURGH Festival of Music and the Arts: 7th-23rd June

BADMINTON Horse Trials: 2nd-5th May

BBC PROMENADE CONCERTS — Royal Albert Hall, London: 19th July-14th September

BEDFORD RIVER Festival: 25th-26th May

BEVERLEY EARLY MUSIC Festival: 9th-12th May

BEVERLEY FOLK Festival: 21st-23rd June

BIGGIN HILL International Air Fair: 8th-9th June

BRAEMAR Royal Highland Gathering: 7th September

BRIGHTON Festival: 3rd-26th May

BRITISH INTERNATIONAL MOTOR Show — Nat. Exhibition Centre, Birmingham: 19th-27th October

BRITISH ROSE Festival — Hampton Court: 10th-14th July

CHATSWORTH ANGLING Fair — Bakewell: 11th-12th May

CHATSWORTH COUNTRY Fair — Bakewell: 31st August-1st September

CHELSEA Flower Show: 21st-24th May (RHS members only 21st-22nd); tickets must be obtained in advance

COWES WEEK Regatta — IOW: 3rd-10th August

CRUFTS Dog Show — Nat. Exhibition Centre, Birmingham: 14th-17th March

1996 Main United Kingdom Fairs and Events — continued

EDINBURGH International Festival: *11th-31st August*

EDINBURGH Military Tattoo — Edinburgh Castle: *2nd-4th August*

EXHIBITION 'IN TRUST FOR THE NATION', paintings from National Trust houses — National Gallery, London: *22nd November 1995-8th August*

FARNBOROUGH International, aerospace exhibition and flying display: *2nd-8th September*

FOOTBALL: European Football Championship Final — Wembley: *30th June*

GLYNDEBOURNE Festival Opera Season: *15th May-24th August*

GOLF — The Open Championship — Royal Lytham St Annes: *18th-21st July*

HARROGATE International Youth Music Festival: *3rd-10th April*

HENLEY Royal Regatta: *3rd-7th July*

HORSE OF THE YEAR Show — Wembley: *24th-29th October (provisional)*

HULL Fair: *4th-5th, 7th-12th October*

IDEAL HOME Exhibition — Earls Court: *14th March-11th April*

JERSEY BATTLE OF FLOWERS — St Helier: *8th-9th August*

LAWN TENNIS Championships — Wimbledon: *24th June-7th July*

LLANGOLLEN Int. Musical Eisteddfod: *9th-14th July*

LONDON INTERNATIONAL BOAT SHOW — Earls Court: *4th-14th January (provisional)*

LONDON TO BRIGHTON Veteran Car Run — Hyde Park to Madeira Drive, Brighton: *3rd November*

LONDON PARADE — from Westminster Abbey to Berkeley Square: *1st January (provisional)*

LORD MAYOR'S Show: *9th November*

MALVERN SPRING GARDENING Show: *10th-12th May*

NATIONAL NORTHERN ROSE Show — Ormesby Hall, nr Middlesbrough: *20th-21st July*

NORWICH CATHEDRAL Pageant: *8th-10th August*

NOTTINGHAM GOOSE Fair: *3rd-5th October*

OLYMPIA INTERNATIONAL SHOWJUMPING Championships: *18th-22nd December*

OULD LAMMAS FAIR — Ballycastle: *26th-27th August*

ROYAL TOURNAMENT — Earls Court: *16th-27th July*

ROYAL WINDSOR HORSE Show — Home Park, Windsor: *8th-12th May*

SAILING: Singlehanded Transatlantic Race — from Plymouth: *16th June*

SHREWSBURY International Music Festival: *28th June-8th July*

SNAPE PROMS — Aldeburgh: *1st-31st August*

TOWN & COUNTRY Festival — Nat. Agricultural Centre, Stoneleigh Park, Kenilworth: *23rd-25th August*

TROOPING THE COLOUR — Horseguards Parade, Whitehall: *8th June (provisional)*

TRUCKFEST — East of England Showground, Peterborough: *5th-6th May*. Shepton Mallet: *6th-7th July*. Ingliston, Edinburgh: *3rd-4th August*

WOBURN ANGLING Fair: *8th-9th June*

Final dates and venues of events listed here are subject to change. Please check with local organiser/tourist board.

NATIONAL LOTTERY

Planetary influences are the basis of the Astro-Guide to lucky lottery numbers in 1996. Any lottery forecast must be fallible, but to give yourself the best chance of winning, choose two numbers from the box given for your star

CAPRICORN
BORN 22 DECEMBER – 20 JANUARY

Money is the root of all evil, some say, but you're far too pragmatic not to realise what it can do for others in your life as well as yourself. Massive odds stand between you and the jackpot, but you believe in your star. Like everyone else, you're only a few numbers away from a prize, and you're well aware of the fact.

| 37 | 39 | | 2 | 4 | 5 | | 8 | 12 | 13 |
| 40 | 42 | | 22 | 23 | 27 | | 29 | 32 | 35 |

ARIES
BORN 21 MARCH – 20 APRIL

Your restless energy won't be suited by just one lottery draw a week. So resist the temptation to over-compensate by buying too many tickets when Saturday comes. There's nothing wrong with optimism however, and this combined with your never-say-die attitude to just about everything could make you an ultimate winner.

| 1 | 4 | | 16 | 19 | 20 | | 29 | 30 | 34 |
| 6 | 7 | | 39 | 40 | 41 | | 43 | 45 | 48 |

AQUARIUS
BORN 21 JANUARY – 19 FEBRUARY

As an original thinker, you're likely to make your own lottery plans. But contrary as always, your gregarious nature means that you usually function best as part of a team. Whether you decide to go it alone or join a family or works syndicate, your legendary ability to be one step ahead of the crowd will count for a lot in a game played by millions.

| 24 | 25 | | 1 | 3 | 4 | | 15 | 17 | 18 |
| 27 | 28 | | 36 | 37 | 38 | | 46 | 47 | 49 |

TAURUS
BORN 21 APRIL – 21 MAY

You always play it safe, and most of what you have you've got by hard work. You'll probably never fall completely under the lottery's spell. But you do like the good things in life, and since you won't worry overmuch if you don't win, why not have a weekly flutter that could pay dividends? If you don't speculate, you won't accumulate. So give your numbers a chance.

| 2 | 3 | | 10 | 11 | 12 | | 23 | 24 | 27 |
| 5 | 6 | | 36 | 37 | 42 | | 47 | 48 | 49 |

PISCES
BORN 20 FEBRUARY – 20 MARCH

Because of your quixotic attitude to money, it's the fun of playing not a real hope of winning that attracts you to the lottery. Vague dreams of lots of money will never be spoiled by despondency when your numbers fail to materialise therefore. This might just be the formula for long-term success.

| 15 | 16 | | 9 | 10 | 11 | | 25 | 26 | 28 |
| 18 | 21 | | 30 | 31 | 33 | | 40 | 41 | 42 |

GEMINI
BORN 22 MAY – 21 JUNE

You will probably bring all your considerable ingenuity to the lottery game, but you should avoid being too much of a system player. There's a lot of the visionary in the other side of your mercurial nature. If you look to the stars for clues, they might well provide you with the inspiration needed to complement that clever logic of yours.

| 9 | 10 | | 1 | 3 | 6 | | 26 | 27 | 28 |
| 11 | 14 | | 29 | 30 | 35 | | 44 | 45 | 46 |

ASTRO-GUIDE *for* 1996

sign and one number from each of the four rectangles. Either keep
to the same numbers each week, or vary the astrological indicators
according to your personal vibrations.

CANCER
BORN 22 JUNE – 22 JULY

Your sterling qualities of quiet competence and
good judgement may not be ideal for something
so risky as the lottery. But you have exactly the
same chances as the next person. Luck changes
just like the phases of the Moon which rules your
sign, and you've never been afraid to reach for the
stars, even if you don't advertise the fact.

16	17
19	20

2	5	6
31	32	33

8	9	12
37	40	42

LIBRA
BORN 24 SEPTEMBER – 23 OCTOBER

Librans of all people are likely to make a balanced
entry, with a good spread of numbers and the
right mixture of enthusiasm and serious intent.
However, you're too easily deflected by others, so
joining a syndicate might not be a good idea.
Perhaps an entry in partnership with a friend or
loved one would be a perfect compromise.

36	38
39	41

2	4	7
29	31	34

9	13	14
44	47	49

LEO
BORN 23 JULY – 23 AUGUST

Nothing less than the jackpot will be your constant aim, but there are no silver spoons before
the winning numbers are drawn, so you mustn't
count too much on the favourable aspects of your
birth. On the other hand your unrivalled ability
to get most of what you want out of life will serve
you well. But don't be afraid to listen to the advice
of others for a change.

22	23
24	26

1	6	7
36	38	40

18	19	21
43	45	48

SCORPIO
BORN 24 OCTOBER – 22 NOVEMBER

Enigmatic as always, the chances are that you'll
secretly disapprove of the lottery, whilst specula-
ting a pound or two. If so, that's because you're
not really a gambler at heart, though you do have a
highly developed instinct for the main chance.
With little to lose and a lot to gain, long odds
shouldn't be a deterrent. After all, you have the
mysterious power of Pluto on your side.

43	44
48	49

1	3	6
18	20	21

8	10	11
29	32	35

VIRGO
BORN 24 AUGUST – 23 SEPTEMBER

You spend a lot of time wrestling with problems.
Temperamentally, therefore, the lottery challenge
should suit you very well. But you do like to be
master of your own fate, whereas blind chance
alone decides the winning numbers. However
Lady Luck is always partial, and the assumption
that your time will come could prove correct.

30	31
33	34

3	4	5
22	25	26

15	17	20
43	46	48

SAGITTARIS
BORN 23 NOVEMBER – 21 DECEMBER

You often need a bit of luck to get you out of a
hole, but winning the lottery calls for such a big
slice of that precious commodity that even your
characteristic tendency to look on the bright side
could be stretched to the limit. Nevertheless
you'll take a straight aim and do your honest best.
Even a small prize will give you a lot of pleasure.

44	45
46	47

2	5	6
23	24	28

12	13	14
32	33	34

Get lucky with OLD MOORE

Football Pools Forecast for 1996

The following forecasts of teams likely to draw on the dates given (allow plus or minus 2 days from the given date) is based on planetary indications and on teams' colours. No claim for infallibility is made. Readers should use their own judgement, but forecasts can help in the final selection.

January 6th	Norwich, Coventry, Grimsby, Charlton.
January 13th	Manchester City, Tottenham, Blackburn, Portsmouth.
January 20th	Chesterfield, Blackburn, Wigan, Ayr.
January 27th	Cambridge Utd., Bristol City, Berwick, Hamilton.
February 3rd	Wolves, Scunthorpe, Bradford, Leicester.
February 10th	Fulham, Chelsea, Bury, Walsall.
February 17th	Slough, Millwall, Tranmere, W.B.A.
February 24th	Manchester City, Chesterfield, Portsmouth, Ayr.
March 2nd	Barnet, Blackburn, Wigan, Hamilton.
March 9th	Chelsea, Walsall, Bury, Q.P.R.
March 16th	Tottenham, Swindon, Millwall, Leeds.
March 23rd	Fulham, Wimbledon, Blackburn, Northampton.
March 30th	Birmingham, Bristol City, Bradford, Leicester.
April 6th	Chesterfield, Wigan, Wimbledon, Cambridge Utd.
April 13th	Scunthorpe, Chester, Grimsby, Charlton.
April 20th	Chelmsford, Wigan, Colchester, Barnet.
April 27th	West Ham, Sheffield Utd., Swindon, Altrincham.
May 4th	Peterborough, Middlesbrough, Rochdale, Southend.
May 11th	Leyton Orient, Oxford, Reading, Arsenal.
May 18th	Hartlepool, Stockport, Newcastle, Doncaster.
May 25th	Newcastle, Nottingham Forest, Bournemouth, Norwich.
June 1st	Blackburn, Portsmouth, Northampton, Chesterfield.
September 7th	Leeds, Northampton, Millwall, Wimbledon.
September 14th	Tottenham, Chelsea, Bury, Ayr.
September 21st	Fulham, Wimbledon, Chesterfield, Walsall.
September 28th	Blackburn, Barnet, Cambridge Utd., Portsmouth.
October 5th	Torquay, Crystal Palace, Tranmere, Burnley.
October 12th	Chesterfield, Manchester City, Charlton, Ayr.
October 19th	Bury, Manchester Utd., Q.P.R., Wimbledon.
October 26th	Bath, Hartlepool, Sheffield Utd., West Ham.
November 2nd	Oldham, Middlesbrough, Peterborough, Dundee.
November 9th	Portsmouth, Barnet, Wigan, Hamilton.
November 16th	Aston Villa, W.B.A., Sunderland, Tranmere.
November 23rd	Chesterfield, Fulham, Millwall, Crystal Palace.
November 30th	Auckland, Arsenal, Norwich, York.
December 7th	Hartlepool, Hull, Rotherham, Sheffield Wednesday.
December 14th	Bath, Cambridge Utd., Leicester, Wolves.
December 21st	Barnet, Oldham, St. Johnstone, Swindon.
December 28th	Northampton, Wigan, Ayr, Hamilton.

YOUR YEAR AHEAD

Day-by-day analysis of 1996 exclusive to your Sun-sign

★ Detailed forecasts, using personalized data – even down to the time of day you were born.

★ Each month analysed for trends in your career, health, luck, money and romance.

★ Full guide to your lucky dates – and how your energy rhythms are influenced by the Moon.

★ Accurate character portrait of your sign with insights into your talents, moods and relationships.

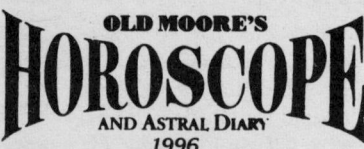

OLD MOORE'S
HOROSCOPE
AND ASTRAL DIARY
1996

Available from WHSmith, Menzies, Dillons, Hammicks, Waterstones, Austicks, Martins and other good bookshops and newsagents price £2.99, or direct from Macmillan Direct Customer Services, Brunel Road, Houndmills, Basingstoke, Hants RG21 6XS price £3.50 incl. p&p.

RACING WITH THE FLAT RACE & STEEPLECHASE JOCKEYS in 1996

ASTROLOGICAL POINTERS TO POSSIBLE WINNING PERIODS

THE ASTROLOGICALLY COMPILED DATES BELOW ARE PRESENTED TO RACEGOERS IN THE HOPE THAT THEY WILL POINT THE WAY TO SOME SUCCESSFUL WINNING PERIODS DURING THE 1996 RACING SEASON.

The favourable periods of Flat Race Jockeys

K. DARLEY, born 5th August, 1960, should be noted on 2 y. o.'s. His fortunate dates are: March 11th to 14th, 20th to 28th (25th to 28th specially recommended), April 1st to 3rd, 5th, 9th to 12th (11th, 12th s.r.), 20th to 23rd (20th, 22nd s.r.), 29th, 30th, May 1st, 2nd, 6th to 13th (10th, 11th s.r.), 18th to 31st (30th, 31st s.r.), June 1st to 10th, 15th to 24th (19th s.r.), 27th, 28th, July 5th, 6th, 12th to 20th (19th, 20th s.r.), 27th, August 5th, 6th, 8th to 29th (16th, 17th s.r.), September 12th to 14th, 20th, 21st, 26th, 27th, October 1st to 3rd, 12th to 14th, 21st to 24th (21st, 22nd s.r.), 30th, 31st, November 4th, 8th, 9th, 15th to 19th.

A. DETTORI, born 15th December, 1970, should be noted on 2 y.o.'s and 3 y.o.'s. His fortunate dates are: March 22nd to 29th (27th specially recommended), April 2nd, 3rd, 6th, 10th to 12th, 16th to 18th, 22nd to 25th (24th s.r.), 30th, May 1st, 2nd, 6th, 7th, 11th to 13th, 27th, June 3rd, 7th, 8th, 12th to 15th, 21st, 22nd, July 7th to 11th, 13th to 15th, 20th to 30th (29th s.r.), August 3rd to 6th, 14th to 17th, 20th to 23rd, 26th to 31st (26th, 27th s.r.), September 9th, 10th, 13th to 16th (13th, 14th s.r.), 23rd to 27th, October 8th to 10th (8th, 9th s.r.), 15th to 17th, 22nd, 23rd, November 4th to 7th (6th s.r.), 9th to 13th, 16th.

PAT EDDERY, born 18th March, 1952 should be noted on short-priced 2 y.o.'s. His fortunate dates are: March 19th to 22nd, 29th to 31st, April 1st to 31st (10th to 31st s.r.), May 1st to 16th (3rd to 16th specially recommended), 24th to 31st, June 1st to 4th, 24th to 29th, July 3rd to 31st (3rd to 10th, 30th, 31st s.r.), August 1st to 3rd, 17th to 21st, September 2nd to 7th, 16th to 20th, 24th to 30th (28th to 30th s.r.), October 1st to 31st (1st, 2nd, 11th to 15th, 24th to 26th s.r.), November 1st to 23rd (1st to 4th, 11th to 13th, 20th to 23rd s.r.).

T. QUINN, born 2nd December, 1961, should be noted on 3 y.o.'s and 4 y.o.'s. His fortunate periods are: March 11th to 31st (11th, 12th, 20th-23rd, 29th to 31st specially recommended), April 2nd, 3rd, 6th, 8th to 13th (10th s.r.), 15th to 20th (19th s.r.), 27th to 30th, May 1st to 11th, 15th to 31st (21st to 31st s.r.), June 1st to 30th (1st to 12th s.r.), July 1st to 16th (4th, 11th s.r.), 22nd to 27th (22nd, 23rd, 26th, 27th s.r.), August 1st (1st s.r.), 2nd, 9th to 16th (15th s.r.), 22nd to 26th (23rd, 24th s.r.), September 4th to 9th, 13th to 18th (16th, 17th s.r.), 23rd to 30th (28th to 30th s.r.), October 1st to 31st (10th to 12th, 22nd to 31st s.r.), November 1st to 26th (1st to 11th, 20th to 26th s.r.).

The favourable periods of Steeple Chase Jockeys

M. DWYER, born August 9th, 1963, should have an exceptionally good year. His fortunate dates are: January 1st to 25th (8th to 10th, 22nd to 25th specially recommended), February 5th to 9th, 20th to 24th, March 6th to 9th, 21st to 31st, April 1st to 30th (5th to 9th, 20th to 24th s.r.), May 1st to 31st (1st to 25th s.r.), August 8th to 12th, 19th to 27th (23rd, 24th s.r.), September 9th to 12th, 16th to 30th (23rd to 27th s.r.), October 1st to 31st (8th to 12th, 24th to 26th s.r.), November 1st to 30th (7th to 11th, 15th to 30th s.r.), December 1st to 31st (1st to 7th, 23rd to 26th s.r.).

A. MAGUIRE, born April 29th, 1971, should be noted on 3 y. o.'s, 4 y. o.'s and older mares. His fortunate dates are: January 1st, 2nd, 6th to 25th (9th to 15th specially recommended), February 7th to 22nd (16th, 17th s.r.), 26th to 28th, March 6th, 7th, 16th to 18th, 25th to 30th (27th s.r.), April 1st to 30th (5th, 6th, 13th, 22nd to 25th s.r.), May 1st to 31st (3rd to 6th, 14th to 16th, 24th, 25th s.r.), August 1st to 12th (7th to 10th s.r.), 19th to 21st, 30th, September 2nd, 9th to 30th (11th to 13th, 24th to 26th s.r.), October 1st to 14th (5th to 8th s.r.), 19th to 21st, 31st, November 1st to 4th, 15th to 30th, December 1st to 3rd, 17th to 21st, 24th to 31st.

N. WILLIAMSON, born January 16th, 1969, should be noted on favourites and 3 y. o.'s. His fortunate periods are: January 1st, 2nd, 13th to 31st (16th to 30th specially recommended), February 3rd to 5th, 12th to 17th, 26th to 29th (27th, 28th s.r.), March 13th to 30th (25th to 29th s.r.), April 3rd to 6th, 12th to 15th, 23rd to 30th, May 13th to 16th all s.r., 29th to 31st, June 2nd, 6th to 10th, 15th to 17th, 29th to 31st (31st s.r.), September 2nd s.r., 16th to 18th, 23rd to 26th, 30th, October 1st to 3rd, 16th to 22nd (17th, 18th s.r.), 31st, November 1st, 2nd, 13th to 18th (15th, 16th s.r.), 29th, 30th, December 2nd, 13th to 21st (14th to 17th s.r.), 30th, 31st.

.. 70 ..

RACING WITH THE FLAT RACE & STEEPLECHASE TRAINERS in 1996

ASTROLOGICAL POINTERS TO POSSIBLE WINNING PERIODS

THE ASTROLOGICALLY COMPILED DATES BELOW ARE PRESENTED TO RACEGOERS IN THE HOPE THAT THEY WILL POINT THE WAY TO SOME SUCCESSFUL WINNING PERIODS DURING THE 1996 RACING SEASON.

The favourable periods of Flat Race Trainers

J. BERRY, born 7th October, 1937, should have a good season with his 2 y.o.'s. His lucky dates are: March 18th to 30th (21st to 24th specially recommended), April 1st to 6th (1st to 6th s.r.), 15th to 30th (16th to 19th, 22nd, 23rd, 30th s.r.), May 1st to 10th (1st to 4th, 6th to 10th s.r.), 17th to 24th, 31st, June 1st to 30th (3rd, 4th, 7th to 11th, 14th to 24th, 29th s.r.), July 3rd to 5th, 8th to 10th, 17th to 31st (19th to 26th s.r.), August 1st to 3rd, 5th, 6th, 9th, 10th (10th s.r.), 13th, 14th, 19th to 31st, September 1st to 10th (4th to 10th s.r.), 13th, 14th, 18th to 21st (19th, 20th s.r.), 24th to 31st, October 1st to 31st (5th to 11th, 21st, 22nd, 24th to 26th s.r.), November 1st to 9th (4th to 9th s.r.), 12th, 13th, 19th to 23rd (20th, 21st s.r.).

H. CECIL, born 11th January, 1943, should have an outstanding season with his 2 year olds. His fortunate dates are: March 19th to 31st (19th to 21st, 27th to 30th specially recommended), April 1st to 6th (3rd to 6th s.r.), 13th to 30th (15th, 20th to 23rd, 29th, 30th s.r.), May 1st to 31st (3rd to 9th s.r.), June 1st to 5th (3rd s.r.), 17th to 21st, July 15th to 19th, 29th to 31st (29th to 31st s.r.), August 1st to 31st (1st, 2nd, 6th to 9th, 17th to 19th, 23rd, 24th s.r.), September 1st to 12th (1st to 4th, 7th, 9th s.r.), 16th, 17th, 21st, 28th, 30th, October 4th, 5th, 12th, 16th to 18th, 22nd to 30th (24th, 25th s.r.), November 6th, 7th, 11th, 12th, 18th, 19th.

R. HANNON, born 30th May, 1945, should do well with his 2 y.o.'s and 3 y.o.'s. His fortunate dates are: March 18th to 28th (19th to 22nd specially recommended), April 4th to 10th (8th to 10th s.r.), 16th to 30th (16th to 18th, 22nd to 25th s.r.), May 1st to 4th, 10th to 31st (18th to 20th s.r.), June 3rd to 8th (3rd, 4th, 8th s.r.), 19th to 30th (29th s.r.), July 1st to 31st (1st to 11th, 22nd, 23rd s.r.), August 1st to 31st (3rd to 6th, 20th, 21st, 29th to 31st s.r.), September 1st to 30th (4th to 7th, 18th, 19th, 25th to 30th s.r.), September 1st to 30th (4th to 7th, 18th, 19th, 25th to 30th s.r.), October 1st to 3rd, 14th to 19th, 24th to 28th, November 8th, 9th, 16th.

Mrs. M. REVELEY, born September 22nd, 1940, should do well with her 3 y.o.'s and 4 y.o.'s. Her fortunate dates are: March 18th to 30th (28th to 30th specially recommended), April 3rd to 9th (4th to 8th s.r.), 12th to 16th, 23rd to 29th, May 4th to 18th (13th to 15th s.r.), 29th to 31st, June 19th to 29th (24th to 28th s.r.), July 15th to 31st (15th to 20th, 30th, 31st s.r.), August 1st to 31st (6th to 10th, 22nd to 31st s.r.), September 1st to 30th (1st to 4th, 21st to 28th s.r.), October 1st to 21st (1st to 3rd, 16th to 21st s.r.), 22nd, 23rd, November 13th to 20th.

The favourable periods of National Hunt Trainers

D. NICHOLSON, born 19th March, 1939, is likely to be successful with his older mares. His fortunate dates are: January 9th to 16th, 22nd to 24th, 29th to 31st, February 5th, 8th to 29th (12th to 17th, 22nd to 29th specially recommended), March 1st to 7th, 13th to 23rd (14th to 16th s.r.), 27th to 30th (28th to 30th s.r.), April 6th to 18th (12th to 15th s.r.), 29th, 30th, May 1st to 18th (13th and 16th s.r.), 29th to 31st (30th, 31st s.r.), August 1st to 31st (1st to 3rd, 29th to 31st s.r.), September 2nd to 10th (4th to 6th s.r.), 14th to 18th (16th, 17th s.r.), 28th to 30th, October 1st to 4th, 11th to 19th, 23rd to 26th, 31st, November 1st, 2nd, 5th to 7th, 15th to 21st (18th s.r.), 29th, 30th (30th s.r.), December 2nd, 3rd, 11th to 17th, 23rd to 26th, 30th, 31st.

M. PIPE, born 29th May, 1945, should do well with his 3 y.o.'s, 4 y.o.'s and 5 y.o.'s. His favourable dates are: January 2nd to 6th, 13th, 16th to 23rd (18th to 20th s.r.), 29th to 31st, February 1st, 2nd, 5th to 17th (5th to 16th s.r.), 21st to 23rd, 26th to 28th, March 1st, 2nd, 7th to 9th, 15th to 30th (15th, 16th, 18th to 22nd s.r.), April 1st to 5th (1st, 2nd s.r.), 8th, 9th, 12th to 15th (12th, 13th s.r.), 22nd to 30th (22nd, 25th s.r.), May 1st to 16th, 20th to 31st (25th to 31st s.r.), August 1st to 31st (3rd, 10th to 31st s.r.), September 1st to 7th, 16th to 28th s.r.), October 1st to 31st (1st to 18th, 30th, 31st s.r.), November 1st to 4th (4th s.r.), 11th to 23rd (14th to 16th s.r.), 29th, 30th, December 2nd to 5th (2nd, 3rd s.r.), 11th to 14th, 17th to 27th (19th, 23rd to 27th s.r.), 30th, 31st.

N. TWISTON-DAVIES, born 1th May, 1957, should do well with his 3 y.o.'s and 4 y.o.'s hurdlers. His fortunate dates are: January 1st to 31st (9th to 13th, 22nd to 31st s.r.), February 1st to 12th (1st, 3rd, 5th to 8th, 10th s.r.), 16th to 29th (16th, 17th, 20th, 21st s.r.), March 7th, 8th, 11th to 31st (21st to 23rd, 26th, 27th s.r.), April 1st to 29th (6th to 12th, 20th to 27th s.r.), May 3rd to 11th (7th, 11th s.r.), 21st to 31st (21st, 28th s.r.), August 3rd to 9th, 10th, 13th to 15th, 20th to 31st, September 9th to 14th (10th to 14th s.r.), 23rd to 30th (23rd to 26th s.r.), October 5th, 7th to 31st (8th to 11th, 14th, 15th, 24th to 26th, 29th to 31st s.r.), November 1st to 21st (1st to 5th, 9th to 14th s.r.), 23rd to 29th, December 1st to 5th, 9th to 14th (9th, 10th, 12th to 14th s.r.), 20th to 31st (23rd, 24th s.r.).

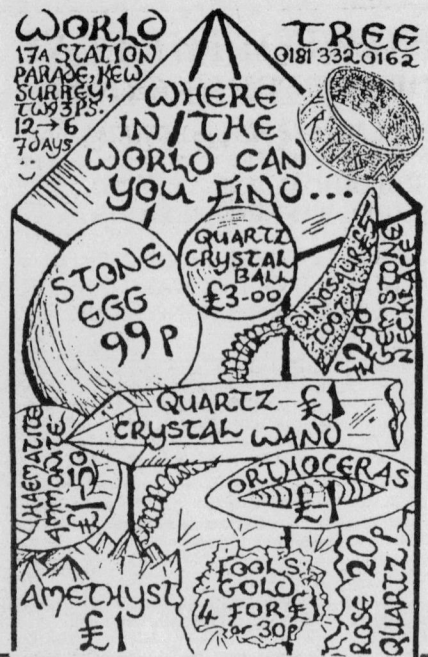
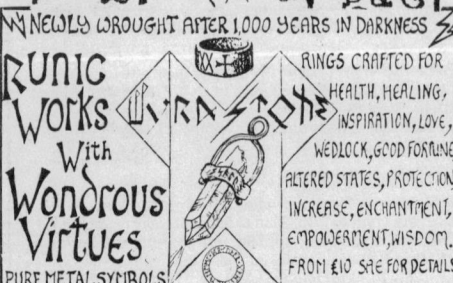

BEST SOWING AND PLANTING TIMES
FOR THE GARDEN IN THE YEAR 1996

WHEN TO PLANT OR SOW TO GET THE BEST RESULTS BY THE MOON

PEAS, BEANS, FLOWERING VEGETABLES AND PLANTS WHICH PRODUCE FRUIT ABOVE THE GROUND SHOULD ALWAYS BE SOWN WHEN THE MOON IS GOING TO THE FULL. POTATOES AND ROOT CROPS SHOULD ALWAYS BE SOWN WHEN THE MOON IS LOW AND BELOW THE EARTH. IF YOU SOW, PLANT OR RE-POT AT THE TIMES SET OUT BELOW IT IS REASONABLY CERTAIN YOU WILL HAVE REALLY FINE RESULTS.

The following dates are the most propitious for sowing and planting in 1996.

JANUARY   5, 6 ..... 9.00 to 10.10 a.m. ..... 12.40 to 3.15 p.m.
               19, 20 ..... 9.25 to 11.05 a.m. ..... 12.50 to 3.40 p.m.

FEBRUARY   4, 5 ..... 8.50 to 11.20 a.m. ..... 1.20 to 4.10 p.m.
               17, 18 ..... 8.35 to 10.45 a.m. ..... 12.40 to 4.35 p.m.

Continue to sow peas, beans, onions, spinach, savoys, lettuce, celery, cauliflowers, carrots, parsnips and radishes. Cut early kidney potatoes for seed and put them in a stove or hotbed in order to start them for planting out.

MARCH   5, 6 ..... 8.10 to 10.10 a.m. ..... 1.25 to 3.35 p.m. ..... 4.10 to 5.10 p.m.
           18, 19 ..... 7.50 to 9.55 a.m. ..... 11.25 to 2.50 p.m. ..... 3.45 to 5.40 p.m.

Vegetables should be put into the ground this month. Sow asparagus, celery, cauliflower, broccoli, spinach, onions, carrots, peas, beans, savoy, parsnips, radishes, etc. Plant red cabbage and sea-kale.

APRIL   3, 4 ..... 7.35 to 9.40 a.m. ..... 11.10 to 2.20 p.m. ..... 4.05 to 5.35 p.m.
          27, 28 ..... 7.50 to 10.30 a.m. ..... 12.50 to 3.40 p.m. ..... 5.10 to 6.25 p.m.

Plant rhubarb, artichokes, asparagus, sea-kale, Dutch-turnips, German greens and small salading. Earth up peas, tie up lettuce, and in dry weather water seed in bed.

MAY   3, 4 ..... 7.20 to 9.15 a.m. ..... 11.05 to 2.20 p.m. ..... 4.15 to 6.00 p.m.
         17, 18 ..... 7.10 to 9.20 a.m. ..... 10.55 to 2.25 p.m. ..... 4.30 to 6.30 p.m.

Sow peas, cucumber, red beet for pickling, and a full crop of kidney beans. Transplant cabbage, winter greens, caulifloer and celery. Hoe and stake peas, water newly-planted crops.

JUNE   1, 2 ..... 7.40 to 10.10 a.m. ..... 12.10 to 2.50 p.m. ..... 5.20 to 8.00 p.m.
         15, 16 ..... 7.10 to 9.30 a.m. ..... 11.20 to 3.10 p.m. ..... 4.50 to 7.15 p.m.

Top beans and peas to assist the filling of the pods. Set kidney beans and transplant cabbage, savoy, broccoli and sow turnips. Thin out onions, leeks, parsnips and early turnips.

JULY   1, 2 ..... 7.20 to 10.00 a.m. ..... 1.15 to 3.35 p.m. ..... 5.30 to 7.35 p.m.
         15, 16 ..... 7.50 to 10.40 a.m. ..... 1.30 to 4.10 p.m. ..... 6.20 to 8.05 p.m.
         29, 30 ..... 8.30 to 11.40 a.m. ..... 2.25 to 6.10 p.m. ..... 7.10 to 7.50 p.m.

Sow turnips, radishes, etc. Plant out broccoli, cauliflowers, savoys, leeks and winter cabbages and earth up celery. Lift full-grown winter onions.

AUGUST   13, 14 ..... 7.10 to 9.20 a.m. ..... 11.50 to 1.30 p.m. ..... 6.00 to 7.30 p.m.
         28, 29 ..... 7.50 to 10.25 a.m. ..... 1.20 to 2.20 p.m. ..... 4.50 to 6.40 p.m.

Sow early cabbages and parsley for the succeeding year, also spinach, broccoli and cauliflower to stand the winter, transplant broccoli, savoys and cauliflower.

SEPTEMBER   12, 13 ..... 7.25 to 9.50 a.m. ..... 12.15 to 2.15 p.m. ..... 4.10 to 6.30 p.m.
           26, 27 ..... 7.50 to 10.10 a.m. ..... 12.40 to 2.10 p.m. ..... 4.00 to 5.30 p.m.

Plant savoys, broccoli, cauliflowers, leeks, celery, pull onions if tips appear drying. Prick out cabbage.

OCTOBER   12, 13 ..... 8.10 to 9.35 a.m. ..... 11.45 to 2.25 p.m. ..... 3.50 to 5.00 p.m.
          26, 27 ..... 8.25 to 10.20 a.m. ..... 1.15 to 4.00 p.m.

Plant some radishes, early cabbages, cauliflowers, mint and tarragon in frames for winter use.

NOVEMBER   10, 11 ..... 8.40 to 10.30 a.m. ..... 2.10 to 4.10 p.m.
           24, 25 ..... 8.50 to 11.00 a.m. ..... 1.40 to 3.30 p.m.

Dig in ground where the crops are carried off and which is not intended to plant again till spring. Shallots are readily propagated by offsets.

DECEMBER   10, 11 ..... 8.45 to 11.15 a.m. ..... 12.50 to 3.10 p.m.
          24, 25 ..... 9.05 to 11.25 a.m. ..... 1.20 to 2.50 p.m.

Earth up celery. Sow small salad in warm borders, covered with mats.

The above times are Greenwich Mean Time.
Allowances must be made for British Summer Time.

Greyhound Racing Numbers Forecasts

This Trap Numbers Forecast may Point the Way to Possible Success in 1996

In the following forecasts, based on a combination of the numbers ruling the area and of the most prominent fortunate planetary number during the period given, the system is followed of giving each area of the country the most propitious dates for that area and the lucky numbers operative between those dates. The first number should be the winner and the second number should be the second dog, and these numbers are printed in bold type below.

While making no claim to infallibility, the compiler of this feature hopes that the information set out below will prove helpful and beneficial to those readers who enjoy an occasional jaunt to the Greyhound Racing Meetings in the particular area mentioned.

LONDON
Jan. 2/12 **3 6** / 17/26 **1 4** | Feb. 3/11 **2 5** / 15/29 **3 5** | Mar. 1/15 **5 1** / 19/30 **4 6**
Apr. 5/17 **6 2** / 20/27 **2 3** | May 1/13 **4 5** / 19/31 **4 3** | June 4/15 **2 3** / 18/29 **3 6**
July 1/14 **6 5** / 20/31 **3 1** | Aug. 5/16 **5 3** / 19/28 **5 6** | Sep. 1/11 **3 2** / 15/27 **4 1**
Oct. 1/13 **6 4** / 16/30 **1 6** | Nov. 3/11 **2 5** / 15/28 **4 5** | Dec. 3/15 **5 2** / 19/30 **4 1**

BIRMINGHAM
Jan. 4/15 **2 4** / 18/27 **3 6** | Feb. 1/10 **2 6** / 20/29 **3 1** | Mar. 3/11 **6 5** / 15/25 **1 5**
Apr. 1/12 **5 6** / 18/30 **6 4** | May 3/12 **4 2** / 17/26 **5 2** | June 2/14 **4 1** / 18/29 **1 2**
July 4/13 **2 5** / 18/31 **4 3** | Aug. 6/15 **1 3** / 17/31 **3 5** | Sep. 4/14 **3 4** / 19/28 **6 5**
Oct. 2/11 **5 1** / 17/28 **2 6** | Nov. 1/12 **2 1** / 19/30 **3 1** | Dec. 6/17 **3 2** / 23/29 **1 5**

MANCHESTER
Jan. 2/14 **2 1** / 20/31 **5 3** | Feb. 1/10 **4 6** / 15/27 **6 1** | Mar. 5/14 **3 2** / 21/31 **5 2**
Apr. 7/15 **6 4** / 17/28 **4 6** | May 1/12 **3 5** / 17/29 **2 3** | June 4/13 **1 4** / 16/28 **5 6**
July 4/14 **5 2** / 19/28 **6 5** | Aug. 2/12 **1 4** / 20/30 **4 3** | Sep. 3/15 **2 3** / 19/28 **1 3**
Oct. 4/14 **4 5** / 17/31 **6 3** | Nov. 4/12 **5 1** / 15/26 **3 6** | Dec. 1/13 **6 3** / 17/28 **3 1**

NEWCASTLE
Jan. 1/11 **4 3** / 19/29 **5 2** | Feb. 4/14 **2 4** / 16/29 **1 3** | Mar. 5/16 **1 6** / 20/31 **4 5**
Apr. 4/15 **2 6** / 18/28 **2 1** | May 1/12 **2 4** / 16/27 **1 6** | June 1/13 **3 1** / 17/29 **5 4**
July 2/13 **1 3** / 17/29 **6 4** | Aug. 2/11 **2 4** / 19/31 **1 4** | Sep. 5/19 **2 5** / 22/30 **4 2**
Oct. 4/13 **3 6** / 17/30 **2 1** | Nov. 5/15 **2 4** / 18/28 **6 2** | Dec. 3/13 **1 3** / 17/28 **6 1**

SHEFFIELD
Jan. 2/13 **3 4** / 15/27 **5 2** | Feb. 1/9 **1 5** / 15/29 **1 6** | Mar. 4/15 **6 2** / 19/30 **4 1**
Apr. 3/14 **2 6** / 16/28 **3 2** | May 2/12 **4 2** / 18/31 **5 4** | June 6/17 **2 3** / 20/30 **5 1**
July 4/15 **2 1** / 18/27 **5 4** | Aug. 2/14 **3 2** / 19/31 **1 2** | Sep. 3/12 **4 3** / 16/27 **1 3**
Oct. 3/11 **2 5** / 16/28 **3 4** | Nov. 2/15 **1 4** / 19/28 **5 4** | Dec. 2/14 **6 4** / 19/30 **1 2**

WALES
Jan. 1/12 **1 5** / 17/26 **4 5** | Feb. 3/16 **6 3** / 20/29 **5 3** | Mar. 5/14 **1 2** / 18/29 **3 4**
Apr. 3/14 **3 1** / 17/26 **5 1** | May 1/12 **1 6** / 15/28 **6 2** | June 2/13 **6 3** / 18/29 **5 3**
July 4/11 **1 4** / 19/30 **6 3** | Aug. 3/10 **4 6** / 15/27 **6 1** | Sep. 1/10 **2 6** / 14/28 **4 6**
Oct. 2/13 **4 5** / 17/31 **4 2** | Nov. 4/17 **2 1** / 20/28 **6 1** | Dec. 2/15 **5 2** / 19/28 **2 3**

SOUTH OF ENGLAND
Jan. 3/13 **4 1** / 17/26 **5 1** | Feb. 1/10 **6 5** / 14/28 **4 3** | Mar. 3/15 **3 5** / 19/31 **4 1**
Apr. 8/16 **6 2** / 20/28 **3 4** | May 2/11 **5 3** / 21/31 **6 3** | June 4/15 **3 5** / 17/29 **1 5**
July 3/10 **4 1** / 14/27 **1 5** | Aug. 1/13 **4 6** / 20/31 **6 5** | Sept. 4/11 **5 6** / 14/28 **2 4**
Oct. 3/12 **4 3** / 16/28 **1 6** | Nov. 1/11 **1 6** / 15/28 **5 6** | Dec. 2/13 **5 1** / 16/29 **3 4**

BINGO
YOUR LUCKY DATES IN 1996

CAPRICORN (BIRTHDAYS DECEMBER 22nd to JANUARY 20th)—January 1st to March 24th, May 3rd to September 9th, October 31st to December 31st.

AQUARIUS (BIRTHDAYS JANUARY 21st to FEBRUARY 19th)—January 9th to May 2nd, September 10th to December 8th.

PISCES (BIRTHDAYS FEBRUARY 20th to MARCH 20th)—January 1st to April 7th, June 13th to September 8th, November 1st to December 31st.

ARIES (BIRTHDAYS MARCH 21st to APRIL 20th)—January 13th to April 7th, May 10th to July 26th, September 8th to December 21st.

TAURUS (BIRTHDAYS APRIL 21st to MAY 21st)—January 4th to March 24th, April 9th to July 15th, October 5th to December 24th.

GEMINI (BIRTHDAYS MAY 22nd to JUNE 21st)—January 2nd to May 20th, July 3rd to October 9th, November 15th to December 4th.

CANCER (BIRTHDAYS JUNE 22nd to JULY 22nd)—January 17th to March 24th, April 20th to July 23rd, August 8th to October 9th, October 24th to December 17th.

LEO (BIRTHDAYS JULY 23rd to AUGUST 23rd)—January 9th to April 19th, May 3rd to August 1st, September 8th to October 30th, November 15th to December 31st.

VIRGO (BIRTHDAYS AUGUST 24th to SEPTEMBER 23rd)—January 18th to June 12th, July 26th to October 10th, November 1st to December 31st.

LIBRA (BIRTHDAYS SEPTEMBER 24th to OCTOBER 23rd)—January 2nd to April 8th, April 20th to August 7th, September 8th to December 4th.

SCORPIO (BIRTHDAYS OCTOBER 24th to NOVEMBER 22nd)—January 17th to May 2nd, June 13th to September 9th, October 24th to December 17th.

SAGITTARIUS (BIRTHDAYS NOVEMBER 23rd to DECEMBER 21st)—February 10th to August 7th, September 8th to December 4th, December 18th to 31st.

Angler's Guide for 1996
WHEN TO FISH AND THE BEST TIMES
THE TIME CHART THAT BRINGS GOOD RESULTS

JANUARY.-Salmon season opens but high water can be a problem. Cold water makes other freshwater fish lethargic. Larger rivers are best bet, with stillwaters generally unproductive except for pike, which will probably feed best on deadbaits. The chance of big roach on bread, ledgering the best method. Chub will feed on most days, and bream in coloured water. Cod and whiting will provide best sea sport with flounders in harbours. Best days 5th, 6th, 7th (A.M.), 14th (P.M.), 15th, 16th (A.M.), 22nd (P.M.), 23rd, 24th.

FEBRUARY.-Snow and frosts make chance of big catches of freshwater fish unlikely, but specimen pike, roach and zander are a possibility. Use smaller baits and smaller hooks for best results. Salmon anglers should be ready for big springers. Cod starting to get more scarce, but fish will be bigger. Still plenty of whiting and some spurdog from boats. Best days 1st, 2nd, 3rd (A.M.), 10th (P.M.), 11th, 12th, 19th, 20th, 21st (A.M.), 28th, 29th.

MARCH.-Sport patchy, but mild days can provide some spectacular catches in freshwater. All species can be caught, even tench and carp. Freshwater season ends in most areas on March 14, with many trout waters opening on the following day. Most trout will be caught in deeper water. Cod and whiting leaving in most areas, but spurdog showing well from boats. Best days 1st, 9th, 10th, 11th (A.M.), 17th (P.M.), 18th, 19th (A.M.), 26th (P.M.), 27th, 28th.

APRIL.-Most trout waters open on 1st. Stillwater trouting will be easy with most flies taking fish, but river fish will be more wary. Black bream showing for some boat anglers, but otherwise sport will be mainly with flatfish and dogfish. Wreck anglers can get good hauls of ling and conger. Some good rays from shallower water. Best days 5th, 6th, 7th (A.M.), 13th (P.M.), 14th, 15th, 23rd, 24th, 25th (A.M.).

MAY.-Warmer weather will start to bring trout up in the water and floating lines will start to pay off on stillwaters. Some bass showing for beach anglers, with crab as best bait, accounting for flatfish and eels too. Good time for plaice on ragworm from harbours. Best days 2nd (P.M.), 3rd, 4th, 11th, 12th, 20th, 21st, 22nd (A.M.), 30th, 31st.

JUNE.-Freshwater season opens in most areas on the 16th. Very big carp, tench and bream from stillwaters, along with big catches of chub in streamier parts of rivers. All baits will take fish, though sport may be patchy on first few days. Bass now starting to show in most areas, and mullet moving into harbours. Mackerel starting to show, and first shark will be caught. Crab and worm will take most shore fish, with fish baits productive on boats. Best days 7th, 8th, 9th (A.M.), 16th (P.M.), 17th, 18th, 26th (P.M.), 27th, 28th (A.M.).

JULY.-The best month for freshwater fishing on both rivers and stillwaters. All baits will catch fish. Sweetcorn and other particle baits likely to prove successful for big tench and carp. Fish will be in the flow on most running water. Good catches of most species will be taken, particularly barbel and bream. Evenings will usually be the best time for trout fishing. Sea trout arriving on many rivers. Summer sea fish well in, and mackerel will attract tope and shark. Plenty of bass, and mullet starting to feed in harbours and around piers. Best days 4th (P.M.), 5th, 6th (A.M.), 13th (P.M.), 14th, 15th, 16th (A.M.), 23rd (P.M.), 24th, 25th.

AUGUST.-Low water can be a problem in many areas. On running waters, fish areas where there is most flow. Night or late evening fishing may be best after hot days on stillwater. Big barbel catches will be made. Sea fishing at its best, with all summer species being caught on most baits. Chance of very big hauls of pollack, ling and conger from wrecks. Best days 1st, 2nd, 10th, 11th, 12th (A.M.), 20th, 21st, 22nd (A.M.), 28th (P.M.), 29th, 30th (A.M.).

SEPTEMBER.-Chance of big barbel, and very big roach and dace hauls on maggot or caster. Stillwaters starting to tail off, but good bream, tench and carp can still be landed. Good time for eels on rivers. Summer sea fish starting to move off, but some good bass still around on sandeel and crab. Early whiting will be caught. Trout fishing now getting harder. Best days 6th, 7th, 8th, 16th, 17th, 18th (A.M.), 25th, 26th.

OCTOBER.-Rivers now offer best sport, with stillwaters generally unproductive. Possibility of good roach, dace and chub catches with caster or maggot as best bait. Float fishing generally best. Chance of big catches of salmon with extra water. Beaches now producing whiting and occasional cod. Best days 3rd (P.M.), 4th, 5th, 13th, 14th, 15th (A.M.), 22nd, 23rd, 24th (A.M.), 31st.

NOVEMBER.-Rain and colder water will make fishing harder in all areas, though fish will shoal tighter and good chub or bream catches can be taken. Feed more lightly for best results and scale down hook and line sizes. Some good pike can be taken. Cod now well in, with lugworm as best bait in most areas. Best days 1st, 2nd (A.M.), 9th (P.M.), 10th, 11th, 18th (P.M.), 19th, 20th (A.M.), 27th (P.M.), 28th, 29th.

DECEMBER.-Although the weather can make fishing uncomfortable, this can still be a good month, though it may be necessary to move around for fish. It will generally be a case of taking a couple from each swim. Chub are a good bet except in coloured water, when bread will take bream. Roach will be less prolific but bigger. The days after storms can bring catches from beaches, where night fishing will generally bring best results. Cod and whiting will be main quarry. Best days 7th, 8th, 9th (A.M.), 15th (P.M.), 16th, 17th (A.M.), 24th (P.M.), 25th, 26th.